Miriam's
Gift

For Gloria —

May life bring
you many blessings.

Warm regards,

Rosemary

Miriam's Gift

Gift

A Mother's Blessings—
Then and Now

Rosemary Mild

FITHIAN PRESS · SANTA BARBARA · 1999

Published by Fithian Press
A division of Daniel and Daniel, Publishers, Inc.
Post Office Box 1525
Santa Barbara, CA 93102

Cover photo by Jessica Frankel

LIBRARY OF CONGRESS CATALOGING-IN-PUBLICATION DATA
Mild, Rosemary, (date)
    Miriam's gift : a mother's blessings—then and now / Rosemary Mild.
        p.   cm.
    ISBN 1-56474-295-4 (alk. paper)
    1. Pan Am Flight 103 Bombing Incident, 1988. 2. Wolfe, Miriam
Luby, 1968-1988—Death and burial. 3. Wolfe, Miriam Luby, 1968-1988—
Influence. 4. Victims of terrorism—Scotland—Lockerbie. 5. Mothers and
daughters—United States.   I. Title.
HV6431.M56   1999
363.12'465'092—dc21
[B]   98-40757
                                                         CIP

For Larry—my husband, my partner, my soulmate

For our beloved grandchildren—
Alena, Craig, Ben, Leah, and Emily

For all the winners of Miriam Luby Wolfe
scholarships and awards

For Miriam's friends everywhere—
may all their dreams come true.

Contents

Miriam, Her Legacy, Her Gift

ON THE day she was murdered, on the day she fell 31,000 feet to her death, my only child left us all a profound legacy. I call it Miriam's gift. Miriam herself would have modestly dubbed it friendship, because it came so naturally from her. But the gift extended far beyond the expectations of any camaraderie I have ever known. I hesitate to call it a "power," because that might sound as if it were forced or imposing, which it never was. Perhaps it was a God-given talent—to animate others' lives with brightness despite despair, with freshness in lieu of fatigue, with renewed purpose to replace floundering or misdirection. She asked only to be loved in return.

She had an uncanny intuition and knew instinctively when to intervene in the lives of those close to her, without preaching, without putting you on the defensive. Her insight earned trust and love. There's no telling how many lives were saved, careers launched, feelings mended, and angers quelled by her interventions. She was no saint, by any means, but her presence emanated endless energy, capturing and holding your attention for periods longer than you thought possible. You did not select her for a friend. She selected you, and having done so, she forged a stronger-than-steel bond between you. Her list of "friends and relatives to keep in touch with at college" contained fifty-two names. But even this list turned out to be partial, as I discovered from letters written to us from across the nation and, indeed, from across the seas.

In many ways Miriam was larger than life—her vision so

vast, her passion to make the world a better place so fervent that her ideals and her joyousness live in all of us who knew her. Her impact on the world was so remarkable for someone only twenty years old that I am still learning new and amazing things about her—and from her.

Miriam didn't walk, she bounced, her luxuriant brown curls bobbing, intense blue eyes sparkling. She embraced life with all the naiveté and enthusiasm of a child discovering her first Lego set—and with the wisdom to savor every precious moment. She was studying musical theater in London. Five weeks before she died, she wrote in her journal:

"The past two days, I've really felt like part of the city—with the pulse of it, the current, its heart. Maybe it's the people I'm getting to know. I'm getting stronger in myself every day."

Until December 21, 1988, I never really thought about acts of terrorism—about the evil terrorists wreak—in any personal way. The murder of Israeli Olympic athletes in Munich, the storming of the Rome airport were abstract news headlines that I read with detached sympathy. But now terrorism has become my own personal tragedy. You see, Miriam was not just my only child. She was my dearest friend, my loving confidante, and truly the center of my whole universe. When she was deprived of her beautiful young life, I was deprived of my most cherished dreams: dreams of my only child as a college graduate, as a mother, as the culmination of all the talent and intellect and achievement she was so passionately yet methodically building toward.

When my daughter, Miriam Luby Wolfe, was sixteen, she gave me a diary for my birthday, inscribed: "Dear Mom, may all your beautiful memories be recorded here and may we create infinite others in the years to come."

Memories of Miriam are all I can cling to now because she was killed on December 21, 1988, at the age of twenty. The plane bringing her home from London, Pan Am Flight 103, exploded over Lockerbie, Scotland, destroyed by a terrorist bomb. Miriam was one of thirty-five Syracuse University students returning from a semester of study abroad. All 259 passengers and crew members died, along with eleven Lockerbie residents on the ground.

How do you cope when your only child has been murdered? Where do you find the impetus to get up in the morning when the most precious person in your life has been taken away from you? Miriam gave the gift of friendship to others. She gave the gift of herself to me. Her strength and *joie de vivre* keep me going. They keep me company. And this is the journey on which I embark each day—to make my life meaningful without her, to make each day count the way she would expect me to. And because it's what I expect of myself.

Miriam was a singer, an actress, a dancer, a director, a scholar, and a prolific writer. Her animated spirit lives on in me every day. I speak of her often—how it was and how it could have been. I do not live in the wake of that terrible day and the terrible way she died—even though I will always remember that it did not have to be that way.

My mission is to keep Miriam and her joyous, bounteous spirit alive for generations to come—and to share her with the world. Perhaps through my daughter you will discover your own child's gifts. Because every child has gifts to give. Yours doesn't have to be an academic superstar or an athlete or talented in the arts to bring you joy. The gift can be a smile, a hug, a kiss. It can be setting the table or offering to wash your car. If your twelve-year-old son comes home with a C in science on his report card instead of the D he got last term, that's a gift. Mostly, it's a gift to himself, but it's also a gift to you, because he responded to your encouragement and confidence in him that he could do better. Maybe your "encouragement" meant some heavy-duty nagging or taking away his TV privileges, but it doesn't matter. You worried about him, cared about him and his future—and he knew it.

Appreciate and accept your child's gifts today. Please don't wait till tomorrow. Because there might not be a tomorrow.

*Miriam's
Gift*

"*I Am a Lover of Life*"

SEPTEMBER 1988. Long before the first red and gold leaves fall from our maple trees, I can sense my usual maternal anxiety dropping away. In fact, I feel that I have almost finished my work as Miriam's mother. Not that we won't always remain close and important to one another. Of course we will. But I feel that she now has the tools—intellectual, emotional, and spiritual—to forge a superb, productive life for herself. I feel this confidence because she's on her way to London in such a pitch of exhilaration. She's been away from me the whole summer. Her first performing job—singing and dancing in upstate New York, in a tiny rural town, at a huge theme park. And she did it successfully.

Her talent and potential are crystallizing. She doesn't just embrace life, she swallows it whole. When we're together I find myself in the presence of an intellect both penetrating and passionate. She's taking on the world of words and thoughts and reflections with an insatiable appetite. She dives into the arts, sciences, and history and strives to master the written and spoken word. In only two years in college, she's grown from a high school honors English student to a writer of essays, short stories, and poems; an actress, a singer, a dancer, a director, and even a budding artist.

After Moses led the Israelites across the Red Sea, his sister, Miriam, led the women in a triumphal song and dance. The name Miriam comes possibly from the Egyptian Meri, which means love. Luby was my mother's name, from Luba,

15

"beloved" in Russian. It was so appropriate to name her after my mother, who was a flamboyant, brilliant, and creative woman.

Nobody can describe Miriam better than she can. She tells about herself in her application to the Syracuse University International Programs Abroad.

I Am a Lover of Life

I am an only child, and because my parents separated when I was nine years old and divorced when I was ten, I am a product of what is commonly called a "broken home." People often expound on the traumatic nature of divorce, focusing particularly on its negative effect on the couple's children. This always gives me pause, because in my case, it was my parents' marriage that proved traumatic. However, my parents' incompatibility as husband and wife in no way prevented them from being wonderful parents to me. On the contrary, they actually complemented each other surprisingly well as parents.

Both Mom and Dad write and edit for a living, and are extraordinarily bright, creative, and warm people. My love for them is so great that it would be impossible for me to adequately express it in words. So, I've decided to focus on what is probably the greatest gift they've given me, and a gift Mom and Dad share: a great love of learning. By this, I do not mean to focus on my parents' prowess in an academic setting. Rather, I'd like to stress that they nurtured me in a way which gave me a burning desire to learn, to take advantage of every opportunity, and to appreciate the beautiful things in our everyday life.

My dad is a compulsive reader—I have never been assigned to read any work of fiction, classical or contemporary, that my father did not own or had not read. So, he was a little worried that I was already seven years old, and was not an avid reader. I loved to be read to at the time, but rarely did I pick up a book and read to myself.

My dad devised a plan of action. Unbeknownst to me, he ordered a year-long subscription to the Read About Me Book Club. Read About Me books arrived monthly, and contained stories of various adventures of *me, Miriam Wolfe,* three of my friends, and my dog!! I was beside myself. I couldn't for the life of me figure out how "they" (the authors) knew all about me. I kept asking Dad the reason, but he wouldn't give up his secret. His only explanation was that the books were magical. And soon, all books held a magic for me. By the time I was eight, I could polish off books with little effort and great joy.

"Books can become some of your best friends, Miriam," my dad would say. "They will never abandon you and will always bring you joy." To this day, nothing has proven him wrong.

Unlike my father, who is very spontaneous and unfocused, my mom is extremely pragmatic and thorough. She taught me the importance of following things through to their completion, and that if you really want to know something, you should take the initiative to learn it. Mom and I used to watch the news together every evening, or read either the newspaper or *Time* magazine—something relating to current events. Often, I would ask Mom a question about something that confused me. If she couldn't answer immediately, I would forget about the issue…but not for long. The next morning, I would come into the kitchen for breakfast. At my place setting, I would find several reference books with little markers in them. Mom would say, "Remember last night when you asked me…? Well, I looked it up, and this is what I found." Mom found a way to lovingly teach me the importance of taking advantage of resources available to me.

As I write this, I am struck by the magnitude of this opportunity to go abroad; to be an active part of a theater community so rich in tradition.

My upbringing was somewhat unconventional in that I never really had a childhood! My parents never treated me as if I were a child; they spoke to me as if I were no different from any of their adult friends. As a result, I matured quickly, enjoying the company of my parents and their friends as much as I enjoyed kids my own age. This has proven useful in countless ways. I was exposed to more than other children, and I tend to believe that self-expression through the arts was second-nature to me because my parents exposed me to such a wide variety of types of music, art, and books.

My parents also provided me with unwavering support. They never tried to dissuade me from pursuing a career in the theater. Instead, they taught me the importance of becoming well-rounded, and not limiting myself. At first, I was angry when they insisted that I not attend a performing arts high school. Then, I discovered how much more I could learn at the wonderful public high school nearby. My senior year was spent studying all the things I had always been interested in: constitutional law, psychology, sociology, Latin, French, and an Honors English class! This terrific year illuminated for me one of the main reasons I love theater so much: the theater allows me to explore hundreds of professions and people, with every character I portray. I am a lover of life, and I try to fulfill that love by illuminating something about humanity through my art. Many students my age feel a need to numb themselves to the pain they experience by drinking heavily or using drugs. I avoid these things. But, my refusal to "escape" in this way is also related to my fascination with the human condition. I know that pain is necessary for growth, and my desires to grow and learn and change are too great for me to jeopardize.

It doesn't take a formal essay assignment for Miriam to reflect on life. She explores feelings and ideas as vigorously as Lewis and Clark explored the West. Reflecting in her freshman SU journal, she says:

> I wonder what kind of mother I'll be? Do I want to be one at all? So many of my friends here have lousy relationships with their parents. I see some moms using their children as an extension of their designer outfits. The kids decorate their mothers like in the English court paintings of the little boys in their velvet suits and lace collars. And I don't want to be an authoritarian figure, manipulating my kids and molding them into what I think they should be. Nor do I want to be one of them—another sibling, a peer. I'd much rather they consider me a loving mentor who gently shows them the way.

At times our own roles are reversed and Miriam turns parental on me. On my fiftieth birthday, when I complained about feeling old, she scolded me:

"Mom, you should be ashamed of yourself. You should be glad you're alive and well to enjoy it." I took her words to heart—her best friend's mother was dying of cancer.

A Syracuse drama professor has described Miriam as "academically in the top five percent of her class.... An extremely inventive and spontaneous young actress." Not surprising—her all-time idol is Carol Burnett. She revels in Carol's insight into human nature, her hilarious portrayals of our foibles and eccentricities.

Miriam's own talent for seeing deeply into others is not a conscious effort; it comes naturally and intellectually, born of her own insecurities. She too needs to be liked and loved. This insight serves her well in her pursuit of the theater. She's a keen student of the characters she plays and has more than a passing interest in psychology. There's a thoroughness about the way she approaches everything. And she scoops up fresh concepts the way our dog inhales Alpo.

"I discovered the most fabulous quote by someone named

Stephen Wright," she tells me on the phone. "You'll love it too, Mom. He said: 'The first time I read the dictionary, I thought it was a poem about everything.'"

Only a month into school, her journal is charged with excitement:

> It's been a great day. In the improv part of ballet class, we danced to a recording of Stravinsky's *Firebird*. The teacher started the music and I was my usual self-conscious self. Then she turned out all the lights, and I was immediately freed! It was sooo interesting to see everyone in silhouette. Before I knew it I was at the front of the room—concentrating completely on the mirror. I lost all my inhibitions, and some really ingenious things came out of my spontaneity. They're reevaluating the placement of dance classes. I'm not very comfortable in the advanced class. I'm hoping I'll be put back in the lower level, where the atmosphere is friendly. I think it would be more beneficial for me to excel in the lower class, clean up my technique, and then move up.

"English was great tonight," she writes in her next entry.

> We discussed Hemingway's "Hills Like White Elephants." I learned sooo much. I only wish our instructor wouldn't spoon-feed us. She has a lot of great information, but I wish she would draw us out through her questions. It would make me feel more productive. We discussed my story and I learned a lot from the class's criticisms. Last night I was going *crazy!* I'd never written fiction before. I was writing and crossing out and writing and crossing out. Now I feel that a whole new world, a new art form is opening up for me.

She's determined to get a well-rounded liberal arts education—despite the possessive schedule of the Drama Department. "I signed up for a history course on the world wars," she tells me proudly on the phone. But a week later, I'm hearing a different story. "Mom, I got to class the first day and—guess what? It's a specialized course for ROTC students. The textbook for World War I alone is 700 pages. You won't believe the detail—panzer division movements, inch by inch. My luck..." she sighs. "I guess I'll stick it out, though." She does, and escapes the carnage with a C.

But it's the arts that stoke her fires. "Berthold Brecht really inspires me," she writes in her journal.

> Brecht is committed to art which serves a purpose other than to amuse. In *Threepenny Opera*, he creates theater which would initiate change. I think the power of his plays comes largely from his "black humor," which cajoles the audience into laughing and then shames them for doing so. His techniques are amazing. His characters stop in the middle of scenes, walk out on long runways and lecture the audience. And he gets away with it! The result is that he enlightens and educates people so that they, in turn, can act out against social injustices. I think Brecht is as much a social worker as he is a playwright. That's one of my goals—to write plays with his kind of power. I want to move audiences, to stir them into action.

So—it's September 1988 and Miriam's father and I have been divorced for nine years. Our mutual anger long over, we are, at last, two contented families—which gives our daughter a well-deserved measure of peace. When she was eleven, Jim remarried—another woman named Rosemary, believe it or not—and Miriam inherited a stepbrother, Chris Spencer. She was thrilled to no longer be an only child.

"I have a brother now!" she told her best friend.

Now that she's on her way to London, I'm actually beginning to relax—for once in my life—not only as a mother, but as a new wife. Larry and I have been married ten months, and at age fifty-three I still walk around like a newlywed. He's so kind and caring that I feel like a cherished bride. I've also settled comfortably into my new job as an engineering writer for Westinghouse. Larry is an electrical engineer at Honeywell, and being in such closely allied industries gives us even more in common.

I've discovered too that I've inherited an exceptional new family. Often, when individuals remarry in midlife they bring emotional baggage and like-them-or-not extra family to the marriage. But not in my case. I'm discovering, instead, how gentle and affectionate my new stepdaughters and their husbands are. Miriam now has two super-smart sisters who are both artists. After our wedding, Jackie said, "It's going to be fun having a baby sister." In the coming weeks, we're to be blessed with our first grandchildren.

Here are Larry's recollections of his first meeting with his future stepdaughter:

We Had So Much To Build On

The night I met Miriam for the first time, she virtually filled the room with her presence. She immediately captured the attention of both her mother and me and held it for the next several hours. I believe that she wielded this captivation intentionally. She was so natural and so wonderfully explosive. It was the highest level of exuberance born of a need to share, to share her life's experiences and discoveries with those she loved. It was a level of animation and energy that could not be contained, for she would simply burst for the lack of its expression. Miriam was a new experience for me. I had never met anyone quite like her.

This energetic and animated enthusiasm extended to every surface and limb of her long, lean, ever-dancing frame. She never stood still, not even for a solitary moment. Her shoulders, arms, and hands covered almost as much space as her feet as she swiftly and gracefully darted about. I found it hard work for my eyes to follow her. Her warm and laughing smile drew you to listen and you dared not let go for fear that you would miss some of the charming and interesting things she had to say. My being there, a total stranger, had not inhibited her in the least.

She became loving family long before I walked down the aisle with her mother. To be sure, my marriage to Rosemary was a difficult transition for her. She felt she had to compete for her mother's affection and attention, and yet it was still her wish that we wed. "Marry him, Mom!" she told her mother. In fact, she sang our way down the aisle with such feeling that tears came to my eyes and a lump to my throat that affected my participation in the ceremony. She and her two new sisters embraced our marriage wholeheartedly.

Although we lived under one roof for only one summer's length and a number of semester breaks, we began to know one another. We both sensed that this was an ongoing process. I was not her father, nor would I ever try to be. I applied for the position of very special friend, and I'd like to think she accepted that.

I was flabbergasted by her strenuous schedule and abundant array of friends. Her correspondence list resembled a corporate mailing list. When I came upon her in the midst of her holiday note-writing, I foolishly suggested that she could be briefer. She replied, "No I can't, they're my friends!" Indeed, these were deep and hearty bonds she shared with so many friends. She openly cared so much about them too. I believe she gave and took in precisely the right amounts. It was a formula known only to her.

Yet sometimes her sensitivity to others' needs almost overwhelmed her. When she hung up the phone after an hour of listening to a college friend in crisis, she herself was in tears. "I wish there was something I could do for her. I know—I'll send her Shel Silverstein's *Where the Sidewalk Ends*. That'll cheer her up."

She talked endlessly on the telephone while pacing through four rooms of the house to the extent that the tethering phone cord would permit. If we'd had a cordless phone, there'd be no telling how far she would go. She left her mark throughout the house in the form of doodles. She virtually obliterated any unguarded Post-it or note in sight, often obscuring messages that still had pertinence.

There just wasn't anything we couldn't discuss, and more often than not, we were on opposite sides of varying subjects. She was an incurable optimist, seeing the world's imperfections and needs as being extremely clear to her. She meant to be a part of its fix'n too.

She pursued knowledge and understanding with an insatiable thirst. Every few days there was a new stack of books in her arms to be read. This she did till the wee hours of the morning, sometimes till three and four, as evidenced by the light from under her door. It was as if she knew there was so much to take in but so little time to do it in.

She was a happy, friendly person to be around. When she bounded down the staircase with her light-colored and tightly curled locks bobbing up and down, I had a strange feeling that she touched nary a stair in the descent. There was something about the way she moved, a nod, a tilt, a shrug, a stance or a glance that was all Miriam. That something belonged to her. Some of it, not all, can be seen in photographs, and that belongs to us always.

So that was Larry's view of Miriam. With all the fervor of a college freshman, she saw no gray or mitigating areas in delineating right and wrong. We were on our way to a holiday party at the H.L. Mencken House in Baltimore. In the car, a heated debate nearly boiled over. I had had an accident and had been cited for reckless driving. Fortunately, the case was dismissed—the other driver and arresting officer didn't show up in court.

Miriam was incensed. "Mom, you didn't deserve to get off like that. You were guilty, you should've been punished."

"You know, Miriam," Larry interjected, "your mother actually did get punished. She got three points on her license and eleven stitches in her head."

Miriam frowned, unconvinced that justice had been served. She seemed to set even tougher standards for me than she did for the rest of the world.

Larry's Honda Accord often served as the arena for our discussions. We were bringing Miriam home from Syracuse at the end of her freshman year when she suddenly blurted out: "My friend's older brother is an alcoholic and he's really destroying her family. The saddest part of this is that he's a brilliant student—he's a senior—and quite charming when he's sober. But she says he's really mean when he drinks. He breaks things and calls her up at two in the morning crying in his beer. I feel so sorry for her. She's asked me, so I go along with her to Al-Anon meetings to give her moral support. The meetings are incredible. I was shocked at the number of professionals there—doctors, lawyers, teachers."

I asked Miriam why the guy didn't go to AA. "He doesn't have to continue drinking," I told her.

"Alcoholism is a disease, Mom," she argued, "not everybody can just quit."

Larry countered with an argument of his own. His first wife died of cancer. She would have given anything to live even one more day. She wasn't given a choice. This guy had a choice to turn his life around and refused to do so. Why should we feel sorry for him?

Miriam protested, "You have to have compassion for people, not everybody is strong."

That debate ended in a standoff. But a few months later, her tone had changed considerably. She wrote in her journal:

> Some of the girls on my floor invited me to a party. While we were waiting for the bus, they kept saying things like "I'm gonna get obliterated tonight." When we got there, I expected a jovial atmosphere. I couldn't have been more wrong. There was hardly any furniture in the house, no place to sit down and nothing to eat. Nobody wasted any time with conversation. In fact, people seemed unable to make conversation! They were chugging down glasses of beer with an intensity that was unreal. I felt like leaving— and I'd only been there five minutes. You see, I'm strange about parties. I suppose I sound snobbish or self-righteous, but I like to talk to people—have intelligent conversations about things I'm interested in. I like to, God forbid, stay sober at parties—to relax and enjoy my friends in a casual setting. Or if I do feel like being rowdy, I like to dance, and sing my favorite songs till I can't sing any more. To me, those things are what make a real party.

At the breakfast table during spring break, she told us she'd gone to a few more Al-Anon meetings with her friend.

"I've decided her brother doesn't want to get sober," Miriam said. "He's pretty happy making life miserable for his family. He's a real expert at blaming everyone around him. What a crock! I feel like telling him 'Grow up, get a life.' I think people need to take responsibility for themselves. That's what life is all about."

One of our most treasured possessions, adorned with a teddy bear on the front, is the card she sent us for our first anniversary:

> Dear Mom and Larry—It is unbearable to be here when what I want to do is to wish you a beary, beary HAPPY

ANNIVERSARY!

I couldn't be happier for you. You both have taught me a great deal about love, and you have an equal partnership that most marriages never achieve. The success of your marriage is not due to luck or chance: you both are extraordinarily giving individuals, which helps you to compromise when necessary. The harmony you have achieved in your relationship spills over into my life, and I'm very grateful for that.

You are both such special people. You deserve the best that life has to offer. And you have found it—in each other. May your relationship continue to blossom, and change, and grow forever. All my love, Miriam.

CHAPTER TWO

Bridges to London

"MORNING, Rosemary, hey, you look beat."

"It's that obvious?" I ask, slumping into my chair.

My co-worker Dianne nods sympathetically.

"Yeah, I'm totally worn out from packing Miriam up to go to England. It took the whole Labor Day weekend."

"She's not going back to Syracuse?" asks Dianne.

"Not till January. She's spending the first semester of her junior year in London. It's a fabulous place for a musical theater major."

"But why are you so knocked out?" Dianne asks.

"Well, she flew in the door on Friday with all her dirty laundry and a pile of stories from her summer job in upstate New York. She was so excited, she couldn't stop talking about it. We needed to go shopping and she wanted to see her friends and our family. We only had three days to get her ready for London. She...."

My ringing phone interrupts us.

"Tech Pubs, Rosemary Mild."

"Hi, Mom!"

"Miriam! What's wrong? Are you okay? Where are you?"

"I'm in London, of course. Nothing's wrong, Mom, I'm fine. We got here last night."

"You sound like you're around the corner. Why are you calling, darling?"

"I miss you, Mom."

"I miss you too, dear, but...." I wait for the other shoe to drop. "How was the flight? Were you bored?" Why am I asking her that? Miriam has never been bored in her life. "Were you able to sleep?"

"The flight was fine. The whole London–Syracuse gang was aboard, and I made lots of new friends. I didn't sleep much, though. We talked our way across the Atlantic. Mom, we found this great flat in Elgin Crescent. It's only a few minutes' walk to my classes. It was a little more expensive than some, but we wanted to be in a safe neighborhood."

"It sounds like you made a good choice. When do your classes start?"

"Tomorrow."

"This is getting to be an expensive call, darling, and it's only your first day there."

"Don't be angry, Mom."

"I'm not."

"Bye. I love you."

"I love you too, dear."

Click.

I flop into bed that night feeling reassured. She arrived safely, she chose a good flat—and she misses me. This thought buoys me up and suppresses the undertow of my other thought—that this is going to be an expensive four months.

The next morning, I barely step through my office door when I hear my phone ring with ominous urgency. I dump my briefcase and purse on my desk and grab for the handset, nearly dropping it on the floor.

I answer. At first I hear nothing and then....

"Mom!"

Miriam's voice comes through louder than usual and rife with anxiety. She hasn't even been gone forty-eight hours. "Miriam, what's wrong? We spoke yesterday."

"Mom! This is an extreme emergency. I did something stupid."

"What? Tell me already." My heart beats faster.

"I was robbed. They took my new wallet."

"You mean you were held up at gunpoint?"

"No! I mean someone swiped the wallet from my purse. I had it hanging on the back of my chair."

"Where were you? Didn't you or anyone see it?"

"No, Mom, no one. We were sitting in a restaurant eating and minding our own conversations. We had just settled on the flat and stopped off for a bite to eat. It was like a little celebration."

"You still have your purse with the Travelers Cheques in it—don't you?" Silence. "Don't you?"

"No, they fit so nicely in the new wallet Larry gave me...." Her voice trembles.

Larry took a business trip to London in July and surprised Miriam with a Velcro wallet sized to accommodate the larger British bills. In it he tucked $175 in British currency. However, the Travelers Cheques that she and I had purchased together were for room, board, and incidentals.

"Have you been to American Express yet?" I ask.

"Yes, that's where I'm calling from, but I need the serial numbers for the Travelers Cheques."

"Don't tell me they were in the wallet too?"

"Uh-huh. Don't be angry, Mom. I made another copy of the list at home, just like you told me to. I thought I brought it with me, but I can't find it. I think I left it in the desk in my room—top center drawer. I need for you to get it and read the numbers over the phone to me."

"You realize, of course, that I'm at work now."

"Sure, Mom, I'm calling you there, aren't I? But I do need for you to go home and get the list now and call me back. I'll wait here for you. I don't have any money."

I swivel my chair around, pondering what to do next. Dianne is studying the work in front of her, tactfully trying to pretend she hasn't heard a word. But it's impossible for her not to. Miriam's bossy side even on the phone always raises the decibels to an embarrassing degree. I wonder how many of my other co-workers are also listening.

"Okay," I reluctantly agree. Never mind that I'm trying to meet a deadline—preparing a presentation for two engineers leaving the next day for Seoul, Korea. I take down the American Express phone number in London and leave the office for home. The list of serial numbers is exactly where Miriam said it was and I call her back. The Travelers Cheques will be reissued immediately, she tells me. This time her voice is softer, as well as a little cockier; her independence has been reassured.

"Thanks so much, Mom. You know, I feel really bad. I was planning to go to the bank right from the restaurant to deposit my cash. Larry was so generous to me. I love you. Love to him too," she says. If she were standing beside me, she'd tilt her curly head and lay it on my shoulder. Crisis over. But after I hang up, I feel guilty (how like me to blame myself). Why didn't I take a few minutes when we were packing to warn her about guarding her purse? We were so rushed that I hadn't even thought about it.

Her first letter to us takes a reflective tone:

Dear Mom and Larry:
The postal strike ended yesterday. I'm relieved. I really needed to get letters off to friends—and family, of course. Yesterday was also our last day of freedom before classes began. It's days without any structure that really start to wear on my sanity. I wonder why I feel so worthless—a feeling of guilt inside about not having seen/done certain things, yet logic tells me there's plenty of time.

I love our room. It's substantially smaller than Christine and Robin's room, but I like it. Our apartment has huge windows and high ceilings—a great place for sleeping during the day like Wyeth's *Daydream* (the *Helga* pictures). The walls of our "flat" are a very soothing cream in the living room, which is decorated in pink, light green, and gray. My room has really light green walls with a bedspread in purply red and white. Jessica and I have matching bears sitting on our beds.

Christine and Robin know a whole group of great Irishmen and brought them over last night! We had a wonderful time—they are much more gentleman-like than American men!

Today was the first day of classes. My classes are lots o' work! Intense! My impressions of the faculty so far:

1. Melanie—very sweet—good teacher, kind woman.

2. Andrew Jack—blunt but endearing! Talented, opinionated, knowledgeable.

3. Malcolm—knowledgeable. Pretty perceptive. I hope he doesn't end up spoon-feeding us, though. So far, so good.

4. Penny—intense lady, lots o' fire. She's like a slow kettle boiling.

5. Sue—politically radical (gotta love it!). Strong-minded, brilliant. A real winner. Political theater is sounding more and more appealing. My book for Fringe theater is entitled *Stages in the Revolution: Political Theatre in Britain Since 1968.* I can't wait to see avant garde theater here!

6. Art History—Amazing self-described leftist prof. She speeds through a lecture as if on fire! She loves art history and wants us to as well.

7. Architecture—my prof. is sort of the second-hander type that Howard Roark (the hero of *The Foun-tainhead*) would've hated. (He thinks the Parthenon is great architecture.) However, he knows enough technically for me to benefit from studying with him.

I love London. I can't wait till I've found favorite places: to spend time, to relax, to study, to dance, to gather my thoughts. I really want to get off the beaten track—meet many Brits, get to know them. Well, I gotta go. I'm off to Harrod's to listen to upper-class British accents. Much love.

•

Only a few days pass before her next call:

"Mom," she says, "I've landed an internship at the King's Head Theater Club. It's a very innovative and prestigious company. They have a trainee program that has produced careers on Broadway and in London's West End and Royal Shakespeare circles."

"Miriam, you're already taking twenty-one credits, plus voice lessons," I remind her. "You told me you and Jessica are taking more credits than any of the others in your group. How in the world will you find time for this? And how about the field trips in Art History and Architecture—won't they conflict?"

"Don't worry, Mom. I'll be working on Fridays—we don't have any classes Fridays. I'll be working the box office and running lines with auditioning actors."

"Um.... That's great, dear," I say weakly.

A few weeks and a dozen calls later, my phone rings at work. This time a weepy voice confronts me. "Mom, there's something we have to talk about." I wait in silence. Now what?

"When I called to tell you about the internship you were so cool about it. I expected you to be enthusiastic and I cried hysterically when I got off the phone." I'm glad she can't see me smiling over her melodrama of *crying hysterically*. But her next words astonish me.

"Mom, we were both wrong. I was working so hard for them and at first I loved it. But after a while they seemed to be taking me for granted. I did miss some class trips too. Anyway, I quit. I wrote them a nice note to thank them for giving me the opportunity." Mini-crisis over.

A postcard to Larry and me....

We went to Wilton and saw this magnificent collection—
Rembrandt, Rubens, Reynolds, Gainsborough, and of

course Bruegel. (I thought of you, Mom—don't you love
Bruegel!?!) We also went to Stourhead Garden in Wilt-
shire—it's the closest thing to Heaven on Earth. We were
all so overwhelmed we couldn't even speak!

In her cards and letters she reminds me of the figures in some
of Chagall's paintings—they float in air just from the sheer ju-
bilation of being. She writes to her new sister in Honolulu:

> Dear Jackie—*Congratulations!* Alena Grace Lau, a
> beautiful name for a beautiful child! I just heard the
> news. Wow! I can't wait to lend a hand in spoiling my new
> niece rotten! I want so much to call you—but the cost of
> phoning halfway around the world is really prohibitive!
>   I'm doing well—classes are *inspiring!* I'm taking, in
> addition to theater classes, Britain Through Architecture
> and Art History! Jackie, we'll have so much to talk about
> when I return!! I love and miss you....

But her resolve not to call her sister in Honolulu didn't last
long. Her next note:

> Dear Jackie—Just wanted to tell you how happy I am that
> you are now a family of three. Alena has some mighty
> strong lungs—I can hear her in the background whenever
> I call. Hey, maybe she'll be a singer! Much love.

Mid-November, another call from London. "Mom, I'm sending Grandpa Saul his card for his eighty-third birthday."
    I'm puzzled. "His birthday was October 24th."
    "Mom, why didn't you remind me?" Her voice is strident
with anger. "I can't believe you didn't. I thought his birthday
was November 24th. I've had his card for three weeks!"
    I'm ticked off at her for talking to me that way, but I keep
my mouth shut. I'm not about to start an argument at work.
    The next day she calls again. I steel myself. "Mom," she

says, "I apologize for talking to you like that yesterday. It was my responsibility to remember Grandpa's birthday." My mouth drops open. I feel like saying: Dear, would you please repeat that while I hold the phone up so my whole office can hear?

By the next week she's moved on to politics. It's her first presidential election and I've sent her an absentee ballot. Another phone call. She needs information on the candidates. I expound for several minutes, quite knowledgeably, I think, but I'm kidding myself.

"No, Mom, I need more than that. What about the congressmen and judges and county council? I'll call you back tomorrow."

"Never mind," I say firmly. "I'll mail you a few pounds of *Washington Post* and *Capital* articles." She casts her vote for Michael Dukakis.

My pleas to curtail her phone calls work only temporarily. She calls my father in Milwaukee.

"Grandpa Saul's not home? I'll call him back another time. But how are you, Hilda?" She chats with his housekeeper for thirty minutes. As the time draws nearer to coming home, her calls to friends in the States multiply like blades of crabgrass on our front lawn. It's her way of reconnecting. The phone bills for her last seven weeks in London: $537.

Miriam showers her letters and cards with exclamation points. For her, life is an exclamation point. With her long, lean frame topped by a burst of curls, you could almost say that she herself is an exclamation point.

In her journal she writes:

Just got back from Manchester Square where the Wallace Collection is. What an absolutely wonderful museum! Fragonard's *The Swing* is there. I could not stop looking at it—it's exquisite. So whimsical. Rembrandt's *Artist's Son* is so breathtaking that I had to look at it for ten minutes.

> Went to Bath yesterday—great city. The bus ride
> there gave me my first glimpse of some of the most
> beautiful countryside I've ever seen. Picture-book scen-
> ery. The grass was so green that in some areas it looked
> fluorescent. Beautiful little villages with cows on the hills,
> and sheep. Bath itself has almost entirely Georgian
> architecture. It has limestone buildings that are straight-
> forward—no ornate crap. The Clean Air Act just went
> into effect there. All the buildings are being cleaned. The
> ones not yet cleaned have brown stains covering them,
> and the clean ones are a light honey color. We saw the
> Roman baths. We'd all like to go back to Bath—four
> hours just wasn't enough time. But I'm so thrilled for
> every moment I had in this beautiful city.

The day after the High Holy Days end she calls to wish Larry
and me a Happy New Year. "Guess what, Mom. I attended
Yom Kippur services at an Orthodox synagogue, but women
aren't allowed to sit downstairs. I protested, but it didn't do
any good."

Of course it didn't, I tell her. That's the Orthodox custom.
"Miriam," I sigh, "couldn't you have saved your feminist cru-
sading for some other time?"

"There's no wrong time, Mom," she says.

We talk about the course she is to start teaching January 6
at the Youtheatre Institute in Syracuse—Beginning Acting for
seven-to-ten-year-olds.

"Have you done any lesson planning?" I ask.

"Mom, I've been lesson planning for a year and a half,"
she says. Teaching is one of her great loves, along with writing
and the theater. In her journal she lists some ideas for the
course and then adds:

> I just learned something about teaching: Never show
> openly, in front of a group of students, that you are
> frustrated by a certain student's lack of understanding.

Don't assume the student hasn't been paying attention. Give him the benefit of the doubt.

A field trip inspires this letter to us....

Hi, Mom and Larry—I'm lying here, in my hotel room in Amsterdam! It's Saturday, so we're leaving tomorrow morning. This city is beautiful, and full of things to do—two days is not enough time at all.

We left on Thursday night at 6. We took a nice coach (they hate the word "bus"!) to drive to the "ferry." What I thought would be a crude sort of boat turned out to be a cruise ship that would've put the Love Boat to shame! It was sooo huge, and we drove our bus right into the hull, where there was a parking lot that housed about 25 buses! The ship was three stories high: it had three restaurants, two casinos, two movie theaters, a piano bar and lounge, and a disco!! It was an eight-hour boat ride. Jess and I shared an adorable little cabin.

Before we went to Amsterdam, they took us by coach to a charming little town in Holland called Alkmaar. It's a quaint place with a beautiful square with two tiny draw-bridges over a canal and lots of little shops. We walked around and exchanged our English pounds for guilders.

Our first day in Amsterdam was incredible! We got up early, had breakfast and set out to see the Anne Frank Museum: the actual annex where the Franks were in hiding from July 6, 1942, to August 1, 1944. It has been preserved, and it is the most powerful exhibit I've ever experienced. Ann, Christine, Jess, and I all cried. The panels in the museum include quotes from Anne's diary (which I've read many times). It's so infuriating to think that this gifted, insightful, articulate girl could have made a great contribution to this world had she been allowed to live. And she's one of six million. It was the most emotionally draining museum in the world.

Then, we went to the Stedelijk Museum. We saw incredible work by Kandinsky, Chagall, Jasper Johns, Van Gogh, Cezanne, and the most beautiful Matisse cutout in existence. It was breathtaking!

We snapped pictures galore while walking around the city. Holland has the most beautiful people I've ever seen—all the people here are blond. The women wear very little makeup, they are all at least five foot eight, thin and fashionably dressed. The men are tall, blond and blue-eyed with chiseled Scandinavian features. They are the most gorgeous nationality! I literally have not seen one unattractive person in Amsterdam!

Being a pedestrian here is a major hazard. Not only must you worry about the insane drivers and the trams, you must avoid the majority of Amsterdam citizens who zoom around on *bicycles!* It's really a charming idea, but downright hazardous in practice! The cyclists are beautiful, blond, cosmopolitan Dutch people who are *out for blood!* We've had quite a few close calls!

Anyway, that's Amsterdam for you! It's been exhausting, but very educational and fun. Mom, you'd love this city—it's architecturally *fascinating*—no two buildings are alike.

She also writes to her dad and his family....

Bonjour! We just got back from a field trip to Paris. We took a bus to Dover (as in the "white cliffs of") and then caught a ferry to Calais, where we spent our first night. The next day, our bus took us straight to Versailles. It was awe-inspiring to be there, but I hate ornateness without purpose in architecture! Versailles is so overly ostentatious; I find it vulgar. But, I guess the bourgeoisie felt the same way during the French Revolution! The gardens at Versailles are a sight to behold, however. The gardens are all organized unique shapes—as though they're meant to be viewed from the top, like an Esther Williams film! We were lucky—the weather was *beautiful* the entire weekend.

We were finally taken to our hotel. My art history professor decided that it'd be neat for us to stay in the area of the city where artists such as Picasso and Degas lived. So she chose the Hotel Pigalle. Pigalle is the most notoriously seedy part of Paris. Our professor forgot that safety as well as historical trivia is important when choosing a hotel! The rooms themselves were nice, though, thank God. Heather and I had a corner room, which had a balcony that gave us a terrific view of the city. We could see Sacre Coeur in the distance, and nothing but strip joints in the immediate area. What a weird dichotomy!

By the time we had cleaned up and had eaten dinner, it was 10:30 at night. So Heather, Lisa and I decided we wanted to walk to the Eiffel Tower and L'Arc de Triomphe. Great idea—little did we know that the half-inch distance on our map meant a walk that would take us till 1 A.M. But, despite our exhaustion, we enjoyed seeing Paris at night on foot. Surprisingly, it's a really safe city. In many ways, it's safer than London! I think I'm the only person to have seen the Eiffel Tower be turned off: they actually un-light it at 1 A.M. We were standing there, triumphant after our walk of miles, and suddenly, section by section, someone turned off the tower. It was actually pretty funny. We didn't get home till 3 A.M. It was quite a long day!

Saturday was the most amazing day of all—we went to the Orsay Gallery first. It has every painting you've ever dreamed of seeing!

The graduate assistant for this art history class is an amazing woman—she's only twenty-seven, but is working on her Ph.D. She is great to go through museums with because she knows everything. She points out interesting techniques unique to a particular artist, rather than just

historical, obscure stuff. I stuck with her the entire time.
I guess I have a lot of endurance, because by the end of
the day Ginnie's group had dwindled to two: her and me.
We spent 4-1/2 straight hours at the Orsay!

Afterwards, we ate at a beautiful outdoor cafe: *le
fromage et une baguette.* I spoke French the whole time!
It was great fun!

We had to leave for Calais to go home on Sunday
afternoon. Sunday morning we went to the Louvre. I was
really disappointed: it was such a mob scene. (Sunday is
the only day that the Louvre is free, so everyone in Paris
was there!) It was so crowded that it was impossible to
enjoy the art. And, despite the guard yelling "No flash"
every three seconds, people insisted on taking flash
pictures of the Mona Lisa. I was livid—these people are
destroying a magnificent piece of art because they have to
have a snapshot (which probably won't even come out—
the Mona Lisa is behind a glass case)!! The best part
about the Louvre was outside: they have trucks that sell
chocolate crepes that they make in front of you! Just like
hot dogs or pretzels in NYC!!

So, all in all, Paris was *wonderful.* I'm anxious to hear
from you (especially my red-headed brother who whet my
palate by writing me a letter!). Keep it up, dear brother,
'cause I miss talkin' to you.

Dear Grandpa Saul—Happy Chanukah! I have only nine
more days before we'll be on the same continent again!
This unique opportunity to learn here in London has
been the most amazing 3-1/2 months of my life.

I saw a terrific play recently that made me think
about you: it's called *Mrs. Klein,* about child psychoanalyst Melanie Klein. I was so fascinated and enthralled by
it that I bought a dictionary of psychoanalytic words.
We'll have to talk in depth when I return!

My psychoanalyst father laughs aloud when he reads it. He gets such a kick out of her intellectual exuberance.

A letter from one of her dear friends bubbles over with the joy of their London life:

Dear Rosemary—Miriam and I were flatmates in London. Your daughter was the most blessed person to ever enter my life—that is what I would have you know, again and again.

Did she ever tell you about Matthew? It seemed as though dashing men were forever falling in love with Miriam in London; while she was working at the theater, she met this gentleman and spent time with him outside work. He was very witty and artistic. She used to go out with him for dinner, and when she got home, she'd recline across the end of my bed, head on one hand, eyes twinkling, and tell me how delightful he was.

The last Saturday before we left London, a group of us went to Oxford for the day. Mir and I split from the group and strolled around the quaint town, admired the extraordinary school buildings, shopped (of course—we both bought a copy of "Desiderata" and an Oxford sweatshirt). We took pictures of children who were rehearsing a play in a church, and climbed up to the tower to see the city. We leaned on the ancient stones, enjoying a breathtaking view, when I spotted a tower across the city I liked better.

"I wish we were on that balcony, Mir," I told her, and she retorted, "The tower's always greener on the other side of the city, Christine." We giggled about it all the way home.

The night we all finished our finals, we went to the Hard Rock Cafe. Miriam ordered a Blue Hawaiian—it looked like Windex in a fishbowl—and we laughed for ten minutes. Her comment was: "You couldn't take someone seriously drinking one of these!!" We laughed so much together.

One more thing—Do you remember a picture of yourself sitting on Mir's bed at school? You are holding hands and both laughing joyously—she carried it everywhere and showed it off whenever she explained how wonderful you are. Love, Christine.

The semester is winding down. Another letter to us:

This semester has been so incredible. I've seen twenty-six plays! My favorites were *Cat on a Hot Tin Roof, Les Miserables, Uncle Vanya, Mrs. Klein, A Moment Too Late* and *Our Country's Good.*

I'm sitting on a bench in a small park near High Holborn Street. Though the sky is completely gray, it's warm and the leaves that are left on the trees are bright yellows, pinks, and salmons. The morning has been quite fun. The Covent Garden/Charing Cross area of the city has all the hustle and bustle of every clichéd song in existence: children laughing, people passing, silver bells. Actually, there's a whole food shop with bells that sound on the hour. I went inside, and the whole place smelled of cinnamon and spice.

Mom, when I get home, can we have a little party just for our women friends? We'll make tea and scones....

The prospect warms my heart. It will be our first party together as adults.

Three days before Miriam is to return from London, she calls. "Mom, I'm worried. I only have an hour between planes at JFK. With customs and everything and if the plane is late...what if I can't make my connection to BWI?"

I'm worried too. "Call you right back," I say.

After making an additional reservation for her on a flight leaving half an hour later, the last one to BWI, we talk again. "If you miss the last flight out," I tell her, "stay at an airport hotel. Don't sit in the airport all night. Are you feeling okay?"

I ask. "You sound kind of hoarse."

"I am, I think I'm getting the flu."

"Dear, get right into bed and stay there. Drink lots of juice."

"Thank you, Mom, I will." I can hear the relief in her voice. "I love you," she says.

"I love you too, darling." It is our last conversation.

CHAPTER THREE

And the Earth Turns Its Face

THE EARTH turns its face the farthest from the sun today, as if hiding in shame, as it does for the winter solstice every year. Nevertheless, December 21, 1988, moves innocently along, with no foreshadowing of the tragic evil in store for it.

Our last workday before the holidays dawns with gray skies and a raw cold, but Larry and I drive to our respective offices this morning in high spirits. Miriam is coming home at eleven tonight. All our plans are in place for her homecoming. After a few days with us, she'll spend a week with her father and his family in Virginia and then a second week with Larry and me in south Florida—days we will jealously guard from time planned with her friends. I can't wait to share my favorite places with her—the historic Italian villa Vizcaya, Wolfie's with its succulent half-sours and blueberry cheesecake. Early in January she'll fly to Syracuse to begin her part-time job teaching acting to children at the Youtheatre Institute. Then it'll be time for the new semester.

I'm swept up in the excitement of the holidays. The world is shopping and partying its way through the glitziest month of the year. Miriam is coming home. It's a time of such anticipation and promise.

The hours fly. Many of my colleagues, already using their vacation time, leave behind an atmosphere of casual freedom. In my office at Westinghouse, the last of the prevailing publications miraculously churn their way glitch-free through the editorial mill. We're packing our personal things and office supplies into cartons to prepare for new furniture that will be in place upon our return. Larry plans to leave his office early to attend an annual holiday reception at his boss's home. At three o'clock I label my last box and chat over the top of my cubicle partition. The phone rings.

"Tech Pubs, Rosemary Mild."

"Rosemary, it's Myrna." Her voice sounds flat, hushed, and without emotion, so untypical of my usually animated younger stepdaughter.

"Hi, Myrna, I don't think you've ever called me at the office before. What a pleasant surprise."

"Rosemary!" This time her voice sounds more ominous. She's calling from their time-share in Ocean City.

"What is it, Myrna?"

"When is Miriam coming home?" she asks.

"Tonight, but you won't be able to see her until tomorrow, she's not coming till eleven."

"What airline is Miriam coming home on?" At first I think Myrna wants to meet her flight at BWI.

"Is it Pan Am?" she asks.

"Yes."

"What flight?"

Now I'm confused. Why is she asking me this? I know the flight number by heart, but suddenly I can't remember it. "It's Flight 102 or 103, I think, but I'll have to check on the bulletin board at home. Why?"

Myrna's voice drops to almost a whisper. "There's been an accident."

I don't ask her any questions. I'm too afraid. Afraid to hear the answers. My heart races. Maybe if I don't find out any details her words won't be real. I barely say good-bye and start dialing Pan Am. The line is busy. My finger frantically stabs at the numbers. Busy. Again and again. I drop the receiver and grab my purse. Moments later, I run down the hall and out the door to my car. I have to get home.

A co-worker calls out to me, "Would you like me to drive you home?"

"No," I say, my voice shaking. "Thanks, anyway. I'm not going to assume the worst." But I do assume the worst. I don't even turn on the radio as is my custom during the twelve-mile ride home. Was it Miriam's flight or not? I fear that if I hear something horrible on the news I'll lose control of my car. I grip the steering wheel hard and try not to think.

I run into the house and turn on the TV. What confronts me is a grim Dan Rather standing before a room-size photo of a huge airplane, the remains of Pan Am Flight 103. The fuselage and cockpit lie on the ground like some great broken dead beast. Sirens and flashing lights pierce the black night.

"The plane exploded at 31,000 feet," I hear Dan Rather say, "over Lockerbie, Scotland." Lockerbie, Scotland? I've never even heard of the place. I turn off the TV. I'm terrified. I'm also disoriented and confused. I run to our bulletin board in the back hall. Maybe, just maybe, 103 isn't Miriam's flight after all. But it is.

Again and again I try to reach Pan Am. Nothing but busy signals. My finger aches from dialing our old rotary phone in the kitchen that we've just never gotten around to replacing. In desperation I call the International Programs Abroad office at Syracuse. The woman on the other end, obviously upset and sympathetic, gives me another Pan Am number that she says might be more accessible. But it isn't.

And then I do something thoroughly off the wall: I start dusting. People will be coming, I tell myself. Dusting? It's irrational, but I don't know what else to do. I don't want to call Larry at his boss's house until I have some concrete facts to tell him. And I still try desperately not to panic. The kitchen clock shows 5:05. The silence screams at me. I feel as if I'm the only person left in the whole world. I throw the dust cloth back in its drawer and pace the kitchen floor like a caged animal, my breath short. Once more I try dialing Pan Am. Both numbers buzz busy, as if to mock me, over and over again. Why isn't Pan Am calling me, why isn't somebody helping me?

Finally, I do call Larry, my voice trembling so badly I can hardly ask for him. Laughter and party chatter float in the background. "Larry has already left," I'm told. At 5:30 when my husband steps through the front door, he finds me huddled in a frozen, crouched position on the bottom step of the stairs to our second floor. My face tells him everything.

Increasingly desperate and frantic, I resume dialing Pan Am. But no matter how often I try, the line is always busy. I have nowhere to turn. Miriam's friends begin calling. J.B. in a forced, perky voice, "Hi, Mrs. Mild, is Miriam there?" Perhaps he's pretending he doesn't know anything and hopes he's wrong; but I think he already suspects. I answer, "No," and I can't remember what else. I will remember everything of that night—and nothing. Many of the details will be horribly burned in my brain and others I will hardly fathom at all. Our closest friends, four couples, start silently drifting into the house. We hadn't called them. A wave of denial sweeps over me. What are they doing here, what do they know that I don't know? But I don't ask them.

By now it is 9 P.M., the time Flight 103 should have landed at JFK International Airport. Still there is no word from Pan Am.

"You should eat something," somebody says. I feel sick to my stomach and at the same time starved, so I mix up some instant oatmeal. I swallow one bite and feel like throwing up. I scrape the whole bowlful into the garbage. At the dining room table several of our friends are gathered in silence, and denial sweeps over me once more.

"Miriam sent us the most wonderful anniversary card," I announce proudly, smiling as if she's just out for the evening. I take it off the buffet and read it aloud.

The hours tick away relentlessly and we are still in the dark. Has Miriam missed her plane? Not likely. Even though as a teenager she had a habit of "running late" (a perpetual source of annoyance to me, the promptness bug), this is a group flight she's on and the students were going to Heathrow

Airport on the bus together. If Miriam had missed her plane or changed her flight, she would have called us. She always calls, she never leaves me hanging. She is just plain considerate.

"Rosemary," Larry calls me from the kitchen, where he's holding the phone, his hand over the receiver. "It's Rabbi Klensin. He wants to know if we'd like him to come over. He wants to help." Our rabbi has been more than a spiritual leader for me and Miriam. He and his family have been accessible as friends and neighbors across the street from us for many years. I push my fist against my mouth and try to think what to say.

"Tell him—" I don't know how to say it tactfully. I'm glad it's Larry who has to deal with it. "Tell him no, but thank you. If he comes it will make it more real." As much as I want and need his comfort, his presence will only confirm my loss. I need to deny the horror of it even if it's only for a little while longer. Larry thanks him and tells him not to come. As a rabbi and a friend, he understands.

By now we have called the rest of my family. In Milwaukee my father was watching the MacNeil/Lehrer News Hour during his dinner, not having the slightest inkling that the news of Pan Am Flight 103 meant his first grandchild is probably dead. He and Miriam adore each other. I hear a long silence before he begins choking and sobbing.

At 12:30 A.M. I finally reach Pan Am. I'm struck by the cold, businesslike manner of the agent; there is not even a hint of kindly sympathy in her voice.

"Was my daughter on Flight 103?" I ask weakly.

The icy, dispassionate voice says: "There's an M. Wolfe on the manifest." Still I cling to a naive glimmer of hope. M. Wolfe is a common name. But then the agent tells me the final piece of information that crushes any hope: the contact number they have for M. Wolfe is Miriam's phone in her London flat.

I hang up, once more crouch down into a fetal position on

the stairs, and bury my head in my knees. I can't cry. I just double up in actual physical pain. "I'd like everybody to leave," I whisper. They're my best friends, but all I can think is, *they all have their children.*

A surge of helplessness and disbelief overcomes me. This can't have happened, this is preposterous. I spent my whole life nurturing Miriam, encouraging her to cultivate her talents, teaching her to become a strong, independent, and resourceful woman. I spent my whole life protecting her, for God's sake. When she was small, I had never let her play outside alone after dark. This summer when I was too busy at work to drive her to get her passport, I sent her to Washington on the metro. That night at dinner she said, "It was a bad neighborhood, Mom." And I felt guilty.

The waiting is over, but the nightmare has just begun, blasting me into the endless black tunnel that will be the rest of my life. Never again will I be able to put my arms around my daughter. Never again will she lay her head on my shoulder. Life will never be the same again.

At 1 A.M. a deadly silence enshrouds the house and I don't dare think. But I don't consciously shut down. My brain takes pity on me and shields me from asking unbearable, unanswerable questions: Where is Miriam now? Is she lying on the bitter cold ground in the snow or in cruel pounding rain and mud with nobody there to tenderly cradle her broken body? I want to scream: "Did she suffer? Somebody please tell me No!"

As Larry and I drag ourselves upstairs, I mentally seal myself off from the futility of these images. I squash them like I squash the ugly, jumping crickets that invade our basement every fall. Heading straight for Miriam's room, I grit my teeth and focus all my attention. There *is* something I can do for her: I can make sure I do her credit. There will be reporters, there will be an obituary. I can make sure that the reporters get the facts right—and there are so many marvelous facts to put down, she had already accomplished so much!

"The media will be calling tomorrow," I tell Larry, "I'm going to get out Miriam's resume."

I find it easily in her top dresser drawer, several copies typed and neatly stacked. Studying the dates, the plays, her summer jobs, I'm reminded that much of the world perceives "the theater" as an unrealistic luxury. But there's a little-known practical side to it, even for children. If they want to audition, if they want to perform, they must put together a resume at a far earlier age than other kids do, because even children's productions require one—Children's Theatre of Annapolis, Annapolis Summer Garden Theater, wherever. So Miriam had been composing her detailed resume since she was thirteen. I set one next to our computer to write a one-page biography of her first thing in the morning and I fall mindlessly into bed.

At 6:30 A.M. the shrill ring of the phone pierces my consciousness. I struggle to sit up and listen to the voice calling from overseas.

"Mrs. Rosemary Mild?"

"Yes."

"This is the Scottish police. Are you the mother of Miriam Luby Wolfe?"

"Yes."

"I'm calling about Pan Am Flight 103, ma'am."

My heart stops. Could there have been some mistake? Could it be that she wasn't on it after all?

"I am so sorry, ma'am," the officer's hushed voice says. "There were no survivors."

CHAPTER FOUR

A House Full, a House Empty

"I PLAN to sing and dance my way through life, star on Broadway, become internationally famous, win an Oscar and live happily ever after." These are Miriam's own words from her Severna Park High senior yearbook. She is smiling at me from the front page of *The Capital*. The caption under her photo reads: "She was a beautiful young woman." The Annapolis area paper has a circulation of nearly 50,000. My daughter commands the banner head and lead story. She's famous all right, but for all the wrong reasons.

We are sitting *shivah*, the traditional days of mourning in a Jewish home. Friends arrive with armfuls of grocery bags and platters. Delicious aromas waft through the house—corned beef and pastrami, onion bagels, bubbling casseroles and apple pie. We won't have to cook for a year. Florists deliver exquisite baskets and bowls of flowers. Food so unbearably succulent. Blossoms so sensually fragrant. How can the dead evoke such *richesse*? I see these generous gifts as a survival technique, defiant, aggressive symbols of life. The determination to crush the stench and agony of death.

Hundreds of letters and cards begin pouring in, many from people I don't even know. Contributions to charities, some of them totally unfamiliar to me. A peculiar state of mind takes up residence in my body. I become an automaton, a robot, a puppet on a string. I fixate on acting the perfect hostess, making sure everything is running smoothly. It serves as a defense to falling apart. In our kitchen, three women I

hardly know bustle about, dismantling an opulent basket of
fruit. One of the women throws the card in the garbage can.

"Please," I say, "I'm in charge here. Don't take things
apart or throw anything away."

She looks at me in disbelief. "I'm only trying to help," she
mutters. "It's the custom."

But I'm having none of it. "I've lost my daughter," I retort,
"but that doesn't mean I've lost control of my life." I retrieve
the card—it's from Larry's colleagues at Honeywell! In a spiral
notebook I record the gift—every gift of food and flowers, every expression of sympathy.

Friends beg Larry and me to let them help and this time I
soften. We dispatch them to the airport to pick up our relatives arriving from Wisconsin, New York, Ohio, Minnesota.
Another friend rescues us from the anguish of calling the airlines to cancel Miriam's flights to Miami Beach and Syracuse.
The phone rings constantly and I hear Miriam's friends on the
other end...friends who were with her in London calling to
tell me how devastated they are. I'm so grateful, but I can
hardly listen—because they are home safe. They live in Dallas, Boston and other far-off cities and took different flights. "I
have to get off the phone now," I say.

A woman friend (to this day we don't know who) calls to
offer condolences. Larry answers. Abruptly she says, "My children just walked in the door from school." That's too much for
Larry. "Hug them very dearly," he says, and sobbing, he has to
hang up.

On Christmas Day *The Capital* honors Miriam with a second front page story, "Crash Victim So Full of Life." Inside is
a yearbook photo of her with other drama club members—
Miriam laughing, arms raised joyfully. Next to her picture she
had written: "Here I am!" with a smiley face. She was so incredibly happy. I surprise myself by laughing with her.

A *Washington Post* reporter calls. My perfect-hostess de-
meanor evaporates and I lash out at her: "You expect me to
give you all these details over the phone? How come you're

the only paper that won't come over here to get this stuff?" The reporter sputters helplessly. "We're going to, but our deadline...." My friend Carol mercifully grabs the phone. "I'll talk for you," she says. She tells the reporter wonderful things about Miriam and the *Post* prints them all. My sarcasm to the reporter wasn't so much meanness as despair, and even as Carol talks I sink into deeper despair. She and Tom have three daughters, our families have been dear friends for three generations. Miriam grew up with their girls, who have traveled on a grand scale to scary, wild countries—China, Malaysia, Thailand, Brazil—and they all came home safely! I send my daughter to one of the most visited and sophisticated capitals in the Western world, schedule her return on an authorized Syracuse University flight on a supposedly reputable airline and she doesn't make it. I myself flew Pan Am from Europe in its pre-jet days. How could this have happened? I rage inside.

As I hand out my typed biographical sheets to reporters, I ache with frustration. How do I tell them who Miriam really was? How do I tell them that trying to set her down on paper is like trying to stuff a tornado into a teacup? Once I told our pediatrician: "She's like having four children in the house," and he replied, "I know." He wasn't smiling.

I circulate throughout the house, weaving my way around the relatives and visitors. Our cat and dog are curled up quietly together in a corner. They know something is terribly wrong. The doorbell rings. Four friends of Miriam's have driven up from Ohio just to attend her memorial service. She met them at Darien Lake this summer. Here I am again, the perfect hostess, asking them about their work and families and what shows they're in now. I go upstairs and dress as if it's someone else's funeral, not my only child's.

We arrive at Temple Beth Shalom for Miriam's memorial service in a raw, biting cold—a fitting climate. As we walk the path from the parking lot to the sanctuary—Larry almost having to hold me up—I see in my peripheral vision high school friends of Miriam's I haven't seen in years; our co-workers; my bosses; and reporters and their cameras—at a respectful distance, for which I am deeply grateful.

Rabbi Klensin's eulogy affects us all. He begins by articulating the helpless horror we all feel:

How bear the unbearable? How comprehend the incomprehensible? Some may find comfort in the idea that it was God's will. But many of us just cannot accept such a theology. No—God's will is that we should live full lives. God wants good people in this world to make the world better, to bring joy, to fight evil. But people have not yet learned to live with each other as God intended. And so a precious young life with so much promise is ended. Yes, even God must be shedding tears over this terrible loss.

Oh, so many tears. And there will be so many more as we begin to accept the reality of Miriam's death. That terribly long night on Wednesday. Waiting for the inevitable news...to hear you answer the phone: No, Miriam is not all right. We've lost our Miriam, lost so much....

We are all aware of Miriam's many achievements in the theater. Many of us saw her act. Many of you performed with her. Her leading roles in Children's Theatre of Annapolis. Serving as President of the Spotlighters at Severna Park High. Receiving an award as best director during One-Act Play Night in her junior year in high school. Winning the Linda Joy Davies Memorial Award for Achievement in the Arts and Humanities in her senior year. Her summer singing and dancing in a show at Darien Lake State Park and the invitation she had received to go back there for a more important role. Her fine work in theater at Syracuse and in London. So many have expressed their confidence that she would have reached the top. Miriam had so many more songs to sing, but that future was not to be.

We have so many beautiful and vivid memories. She was a young girl of seven when my wife and I moved in across the street from Miriam and her family. Watching her grow. Always running, always busy, always smiling. And the memories in this sanctuary. As I stood here with her at Confirmation. Asking God's blessing upon her for a full, happy, and successful life. And especially the vivid image of Miriam standing right here singing at the wedding ceremony for her mother and Larry. So beautiful, so sincere. None of us could keep in the tears. But those were tears of joy. So much joy she brought to the lives of so many.

Miriam was an idealist who cared deeply about our world and the pain and suffering of others. And she wouldn't listen when anyone told her that one cannot deal with it all. She knew it was her responsibility to correct the wrongs of the world. She couldn't understand how others ignore the evil and suffering around them. She wanted to feed the hungry, clothe the naked, house the homeless. She expressed this concern as a child collecting for UNICEF and getting others to do so. In London forming a new theater group to bring back to Syracuse that would perform plays on such issues as rape and AIDS. One of her teachers said she responded fully despite any consequences, even to the point of Thoreau-like disobedience. Her grandmother just received a card from her, one of the last Miriam wrote before she died, and it contained a quotation from Ghandi: "The world has enough for every man's need, but not enough for every man's greed."

Miriam took the time for what was important. She served for two years as co-president of our temple Youth Group and by virtue of that position, as a trustee on our congregational board of directors.

There are so many adjectives we hear to describe Miriam and all of them so true—they are an alphabet of praise and respect: She was affirmative and accomplished, bright and bubbly, creative, caring, charismatic and

compassionate, dependable, enthusiastic, friendly and
funny, gifted and giving, hurrying, insightful and inspir-
ing, joyous, kind, loving, a listener, motivated and moti-
vating, nurturing, observant, positive, questioning, radiant, sensitive, thoughtful, understanding, vibrant, vital,
and vivacious. Miriam was a wonderful young woman.

I want to share with you part of a letter which one of
Miriam's high school teachers wrote to me:

"Thousands of students have passed through my
classroom; a few have left behind such durable impressions that I can conjure pictures of their faces, remember
what their ambitions were, where they sat, what their
handwriting looked like, and what our standard jokes
were. Not only was Miriam such a student, but she
returned many times after she went to college and became a friend.

"She loved words and people and movement. Seen
superficially, such passion would seem naturally to lead
her to acting and theater; but these loves were more a
way of living. When she came back to visit us after going
to Syracuse, she wanted to reminisce and talk about the
new things she had learned, about her successes and trials
in the student theater, about the books she had read here
and was now reading from a different point of view, about
her latest discoveries in people and ideas, about people at
college who were just like some of us or perhaps, more
mercifully, not like us at all. Conversations with her were
far ranging and punctuated with funny and extravagant
gestures and grins. Always her enthusiasms came trailing
laughter and arrayed in smiles. And that is how I will
remember her, bursting through the door, hair curling
around her face, arms extended to embrace everyone, the
very essence of vitality and joy."

How can we make sense of this tragedy? We can't.
But we must not give victory to those who would destroy
life. Miriam wanted to give life. We must carry on for her.

Our response must be to do what she would have done.
To help someone; to right a wrong; to raise consciousness;
and to smile. To smile, not today nor tomorrow, maybe
not next week—it will take a while. But in time, to smile
Miriam's smile for her, to bring some joy. That is what
Miriam would have given to us. And as our grief grows
dull, to look around and appreciate the world as she
would have—as she taught us to do, and so she will go on
living through us. Miriam will live on through us. *Zecher
tzadeket livracha.* The memory of the righteous shall be a
blessing.

Back at our house, jammed with people after the service, I
play my role. I'm considerate of everyone, offering sandwiches. Miriam's Ohio friends put on their jackets. "I have to get
back for work," Jody tells me. And in the flash of a heartbeat, I
assume her own mother's role: "You have a long trip. Drive
carefully, that's the most important thing," I say. Once a mother, always a mother. It's a reflex action. But a moment later I'm
choking up at the sight of my pretty, blond nineteen-year-old
niece and my teenage cousins. They all look so healthy! I listen to the dozen young people crowded into our living room
talking quietly about their lives—making the honor roll, or
having trouble with Spanish; finding jobs or changing jobs;
getting married or breaking engagements. Just...breathing.

Miriam's friends Bonnie and Pete come in the door carrying a huge evergreen wreath. Attached to it are sentimental
items from Severna Park High drama club members, including one of Bonnie's first ballet slippers and a poem. They all
performed together in *You Can't Take It With You*. The poem
was composed on the ancient typewriter that was Miriam's
prop when she played the zany Penny Sycamore.

Tomorrow Pete, a licensed private pilot, and Bonnie will
take the wreath up in a plane and drop it over the Chesapeake
Bay, a salute to Miriam, who so loved Annapolis and the Bay.

One of our young women visitors hands me a box containing an American flag and a certificate: "This flag was flown over the United States Capitol on December 21, 1988, at the request of the Honorable Henry J. Nowak. This flag will be presented to the parents of Miriam Wolfe." Karen works for Congressman Nowak, who represents a New York state district including Syracuse. In happier times, Karen and Miriam performed in Children's Theatre of Annapolis together.

"We'll fly the flag," I promise her. "Every Memorial Day and Fourth of July."

Certificates pour in from the Jewish National Fund. More than forty trees have been planted in Israel in Miriam's memory. I suddenly remember a certificate arriving in the mail ten years ago addressed to "Shane Henry Wolfe"—Miriam's dog. "Dear Sir: A tree has been planted in your honor in the Jewish National Forest in Israel." She had arranged it through her religious school class.

"Some day," my five-year-old daughter once told me, "I'll be able to climb all the trees I want." Looking back, her words seemed to be the beginning of a whole approach to life: that there was nothing in the world she couldn't do—and she started right in! She came home from kindergarten and announced: "Mom, there's going to be a science fair, and I'm going to grow an apple tree from a seed."

Was this even possible? I cut open a Red Delicious apple and rustled up half a bag of potting soil from under the sink. A few weeks later, the seeds sprouted. After the science fair ended, she planted the sprouts in the backyard. A straggly apple tree grew—and even grew bushy. And seven years later, it bore its first apples. I was ecstatic.

"Miriam, you've made yourself immortal!" Little did I know how prophetic I was. But she wasn't much impressed. For her it was routine, her typical *modus operandi* of giving something to the world. The tree continues to work its magic. A few Augusts ago, our grandchildren ecstatically plucked the apples, and Jackie and Myrna baked two pies.

I've discovered a remarkable coincidence: Miriam was

born on September 26. And so was John Chapman—better known as Johnny Appleseed, that marvelous pioneer who walked the countryside planting apple trees.

She wrote this poem to her apple tree when she was fifteen:

> **My Special Tree**
> With each new season I awake
> From my preoccupation;
> And wonder if my tree has changed
> Whilst I practiced hibernation.
> It's time for my awakening
> To see God's gift to me.
> Then I stroll out front to my friend,
> A very special tree
> (Which has many a pleasant memory)
> And enjoy a soothingly ecstatic dose
> Of God's own gift to me,
> My very own special tree.

A majestic maple tree dominates our front yard, and sometimes, when Miriam and I had an argument, she'd run outside and I'd know just where to find her. I'd look up and there would be two sneakers peeking out through the leaves. She'd be sitting up there, cooling off. Her love of trees lasted her whole life; she even taught a friend to climb one in London.

I stare out the kitchen window at Miriam's bare apple tree silhouetted against the December dusk. As night falls and the house empties, our exhausted family members bedding down upstairs, I feel the ghostly silence. I move away from the window. Miriam isn't coming home. God gave her to me for twenty years. How will I survive without her?

And I feel defenseless and deeply threatened. Her plane exploded. I want to lash out and wreak vengeance on the powerful evil forces that have stolen my daughter from me. But who and where is the enemy?

CHAPTER FIVE

A *Pebble in My Pocket*

SOMEBODY switches on the TV. Anxious family members cluster in the living room. A cereal commercial blares, interfering with any prospect of news about the bombing of Miriam's plane. It's Christmas Day. Then the kindly face of Charles Kuralt fills the screen. He devotes his program *Sunday Morning* to Pan Am Flight 103, including an interview with a State Department expert on counterterrorism. Suddenly, an amazing thing happens. Mr. Kuralt finishes his program this way:

> It is hard to think of large numbers of disaster victims as individuals, but we should try. We received this letter just before Christmas. It comes to us from Kenneth Bolinsky of Sellersville, Pennsylvania. It says:
> "Dear Mr. Kuralt:
> "In the folklore of Eastern European Jewry is found the tale of the Tzaddikim—thirty-six holy good souls upon whose existence lies the responsibility for the balance of good and evil in the universe. The Tzaddik is, however, totally unaware of this burden.
> "I am writing to tell you of one such soul. During my three years of graduate study at Syracuse University she became a part of my days—a soothing moment in passing. She was a blissfully talented creature full of joy and of light and of love. She was my friend. There is now a serious imbalance in the universe: Miriam Wolfe was aboard Pan Am Flight 103. I thought you'd want to know."

Of all the passengers on the plane, it is my daughter Mr. Kuralt chooses to talk about, and I ask myself whether I have understood my child too little; whether I have paid too little attention. In April 1989 I write to Ken Bolinsky to thank him for honoring Miriam's memory. Here is his reply:

Dear Mr. and Mrs. Mild:

I got to know Miriam through other friends: I chose to share their grief at her loss, not recognizing my own. We are a strange animal, not always knowing when we have been wounded and, even then, not how deeply. I wrote the letter to Mr. Kuralt out of a sense of fear, of emptiness—I had to share my anxiety. The writing was my catharsis. I cannot tell you why I sent the letter to him—I'm not certain that I know. Perhaps because I have come to trust him. I marked it "Personal" and never expected a response in any form.

I heard the words I had written while preparing my family's Christmas breakfast and found myself crying again. What followed, though, was something wonderful: As the broadcast made its way across the country, distant friends called to share their frustration at the horror that had befallen us all. Miriam allowed us to touch, and ease, our mutual pain. How like her to help others, to help strangers find a healing peace.

Perhaps that is the memory of your daughter that stays with me: I keep it like a smooth, bright pebble— safe in the bottom of a pocket.

CHAPTER SIX

Footprints

"I'M YOUR Pan Am representative, Rosemary," the deep voice on the phone announces. "Each Flight 103 family has been assigned one."

Miriam has been dead for two or three days and this is Pan Am's first effort to contact me. And he's calling me by my first name—how dare he?

I'm civil, but from the very first moment of contact our relationship festers. He talks and I hear noise in the background. "I'm calling you from home," he says. "That's my two-year-old son." (This is not a good beginning.)

"I want to explain to you what's going on in Lockerbie. The Scottish police are in the process of identifying the Flight 103 passengers. What you will need to do, Rosemary, is provide us with documentation to help identify Miriam's body."

Identify Miriam's body. His words rip through me, and a terrible realization sets in. The explosion killed 270 people and the authorities don't even know which one of them is my daughter. At this moment she has no identity at all. My beautiful and loving child. I want to challenge this Pan Am person, attack him, shout at him: What have you done with her? Where is she now? And what if they can't identify her? But I seal myself off from my inner hysteria. If I dwell on these thoughts, I know I'll stop functioning. I've been given an assignment; in school I always conscientiously completed my assignments.

But I can't seal myself off from the world. It's the holidays.

Today my friends are browsing through the malls with *their* daughters, shopping for bargains.

On January 2, the doorbell rings. A dark-haired man of medium height stands on our porch.

"FBI Special Agent Robert Saunders." His voice is deferential.

I hold the door for him. A chill shoots through me. Even though Larry and I are expecting him, there's something frightening about an official appointment with the Federal Bureau of Investigation. Because Pan Am 103 was an international incident, the FBI is working with the Scottish police and American Consulate in Edinburgh.

Sitting next to him on our living room couch, I can see that Mr. Saunders is a sensitive man who almost feels he is intruding on us. But I know why he's here. He has come to collect items that might contain Miriam's fingerprints.

The first thing he does is fingerprint Larry and me so the authorities will be able to distinguish Miriam's prints from ours. This act in itself is unnatural—it makes me feel like a criminal. The procedure done, I know what's expected of me and I'm prepared. For two days I've been roaming through the house asking myself what I can give the FBI that will help identify my child.

All the items I've gathered sit before us on the coffee table. They looked so forlorn, so pathetic, almost as if I'm invading Miriam's privacy. Trembling, I silently hand him my treasures. A jar of strawberry jam with a red-flowered calico cover and red yarn ribbon; Miriam made the jam for me this summer at Darien Lake—it was one of my birthday presents. A bottle of her shampoo. Cans of her mousse and shaving cream. A brochure she sent us from King's Head Theatre, where she interned in London. *A Practical Handbook for the Actor*—a gift from a Syracuse faculty member and friend. I also feel compelled to give the agent photographs: Miriam and me in our brown vinyl recliner, where we used to cozily squeeze in together to watch *Dallas* on Friday nights; three pictures of herself that she sent us only two weeks ago. She wore such a joyous smile, with her mass of curls flying in the breeze, against a background of a castle in Wales, a canal and windmills in Amsterdam. This was the way it was supposed to be. My jubilant daughter drinking in all of life.

Suddenly, my brain shifts into overdrive as a rush of memory takes me back to the hospital in Washington, D.C., where Miriam was born. I remember a nurse handing me a large white certificate containing my baby's footprints. But will I be able to find it after twenty years? I hurry out of the room and take the stairs two at a time. And there it is, nestled precisely in the medical folder where I had stored it. But what do I know about a newborn's footprints? Are they the same twenty years later? I don't even ask Mr. Saunders whether he can use this document—I just have to give it to him. He seems to understand. "Thank you," he says. "Everything will be returned to you." Our appointment is over.

Days pass in pounding rain and wind-whipped snow. Larry and I want answers, we want advice, but we do not know who in officialdom to turn to.

The phone rings. "It's the State Department!" Larry shouts upstairs to me. At last! But my first reaction is resentment and anger. Where has my government been all this time? Pan Am 103 exploded over a foreign country. Why wasn't the State Department there for us the night Miriam died? Like Pan Am, the State Department has assigned a liaison to assist each of the families. I get a gentle lady, eager to help, a Ms. Waters.

But peace of mind—in fact, any respite at all—is not to come. Instead, my days earthquake from one shock to another. My Pan Am representative rings me up, quite matter of fact and brisk. "The authorities are still working on identifying Miriam's body," he tells me. "Would you please pick up Miriam's dental records from her dentist and orthodontist?"

How can he ask me to do such a thing? And why do they need such records? Isn't my jar of strawberry jam enough? A wave of nausea overtakes me as I visualize myself walking jauntily into the dental offices: "Hi, there! May I trouble you to hand over my daughter's dental records so her body can be identified?" I grab the phone and call Ms. Waters. Her momentary silence tells me she is stunned, and then she calms me.

"Of course, you don't have to do it. You should never have been asked. I will send a courier from the State Department."

"Police Scour Crash Site Like Crime Scene." Within three days they know it was sabotage—a bomb. My head nearly explodes with questions. How could a bomb have gotten on board? Why didn't Pan Am discover it? What about the Federal Aviation Administration? The FAA is supposed to have strict procedures to prevent a bomb from getting past security at an airport. Why didn't Pan Am protect my child and the other passengers? Why didn't my government protect them?

Fresh malevolent news stories seep into the papers. Two weeks before Miriam's plane exploded, the United States government received a warning that a terrorist attack was to be launched against Pan Am. The attack would take place within a two-week period in December, the approximate time frame of Miriam's flight! Did the government warn Pan Am? And if so, why hadn't Pan Am warned its passengers? My worst nightmare is now confirmed: this calamity, this tragedy could have been prevented.

It is now sixteen days since Miriam's death—January 6—and I return to my job at Westinghouse. The engineer for whom I'm preparing a briefing sits down next to my desk and opens his briefcase.

"I'm surprised you're back so soon," he says. I consciously press my lips together so I won't say something I'll regret.... Am I breaking the rules for grieving, sir? Or are you going to invent new ones for me—perhaps *Miss Manners' Guide to Excruciatingly Correct Mourning.*

But I smother my anger, suppress my sarcasm as he spreads out his papers on my desk. I have come back to work quickly because it is my only salvation. If I stay home even one more day I will spend every waking moment crying, pacing from room to room; or worse, pacing obsessively in Miriam's room.

But let's be fair. The Westinghouse engineer, a retired Air Force colonel, is not trying to shame me—and deep down I know it. He's merely trying to express some depth of understanding of my tragedy.

My fellow engineering writers treat me with sensitivity and kindness. One organizes an office collection of contributions to our newly formed Miriam Luby Wolfe Scholarship Fund at temple. Other co-workers reveal tragic times in their own lives: Debbie's young fiancé killed on his motorcycle; Gloria's teenage son dead in a car crash.

My bosses tell me to take as much time off as I need to. Actually, I will take very little. Being at work gives focus to my life and makes me feel worthwhile. As best I can, I compartmentalize myself so I can function and work. Sometimes it helps, often it doesn't. In my corner cubicle I gratefully face the wall, where my designated space provides protection and refuge. But in truth, I want to zip myself up into a warm, dark sleeping bag. Head and all. Forever. Because now I'm different from all my co-workers. I have lost my only child. Now I'm maimed, no longer a whole person. And now that I've lost Miriam, am I no longer a mother? I'm a much-loved stepmom, but am I still a mother? I feel like I am. But what do other people think? I don't know. I hear a co-worker chatter about his children.

"They're growing up," he says. "They always do." No sir, they don't. Some of them don't get to. I feel like a leper—somehow no longer a normal part of the mainstream of humanity.

And back at work I discover that most of my colleagues feel uncomfortable when I talk about Miriam. They glance around the room uneasily, hoping I'll stop soon. Dianne is the exception. She listens to me for hours, sometimes with tears in her eyes. She and her husband brought their boys, ages three and eight, to our house for a condolence call. Knowing that their family takes many plane trips, I ask her: "Did you tell your kids the truth about how Miriam died?"

"Oh, yes," she says, "I never lie to my children."

In my cubicle I start editing a booklet on the new radar technology to be installed in major U.S. airports. But I can't focus. I'm still bruised from yesterday—the unavoidable visit to my lawyer's office to take care of official business: Miriam's death certificate. The moment I saw it I wept uncontrollably. The black and white reality of it. Miriam's body was *"found December 24."* December 24! She was lying out on the cold winter ground in Scotland for three days.

And sitting in the lawyer's office, another reality hit me: I now have to rewrite my will. My family line of inheritance is broken. All our family's sentimental belongings that Miriam would have treasured will now be meaningless—the Royal Worcester china, custom-designed for my parents in England; a sterling silver samovar dated 1872, inherited from my grandparents; my entire library. And in our basement storage closet sit cartons that Larry and I have lovingly filled—overflow items from our two households for Miriam's first apartment after college. Dishes, silverware, wine glasses, bright tablecloths. More evidence of our high hopes for her happiness.

The phone jangles. It must be my customer calling about his radar brochure. But it's not. It's my Pan Am liaison.

"I have news, Rosemary. Miriam's body has been identified. It's being shipped to Dulles International Airport in Virginia in two days."

I can't stay in the office another minute. I lay down my pencil, grab my coat and, without a word, head for home.

Jim and Rosemary go to Dulles to receive Miriam's body. Late that night, Larry and I wait to receive it at the funeral home in Annapolis, where we face the wrenching task of choosing a coffin. But there is a more immediate nightmare to attend to. Somebody has to officially identify Miriam's body at the funeral home. Larry offers, and we put in a call to Jim to discuss it. He says no: "It would be unfair for Larry to have to carry that memory with him."

Rabbi Klensin comes to the rescue and we gratefully accept. He meets us at the funeral home and, after making the identification, tells us, "Yes, it's Miriam, but you don't want to see her." I take his word for it.

"We do have one 'blessing,' if you can call it that," Larry says. "We can always remember Miriam the way she was, at the peak of her beauty." Blooming and radiant, with her intense, all-seeing blue eyes, her gorgeous smile, her lilting laugh and bouncing walk, her willowy five-foot-five frame. Larry lost his first wife to a lingering cancer and I carry with me the same images he does—my pretty young mother dying of cancer. It's been more than forty years and I still can't block from my mind her last withered months.

At the funeral home we choose the coffin, a burnished walnut, and I sit down in a corner to reflect. Several times during her college years, Miriam quoted this little poem by Zoe Atkins:

So much do I love wandering,
So much I love the sea and sky,
That it will be a piteous thing
In one small grave to lie.

What prompted Miriam to cite this poem so often? Was it a terrible premonition? Life was so precious to her, and now, lifetimes before her time, she lies in a piteous grave.

Not many teenagers give a thought to how the Hereafter will remember them. They think themselves invincible—they're gonna live forever. In Miriam's Honors English class at Severna Park High, students were asked to describe the tombstone they would want for themselves and write their epitaph. At age fifteen, this is what she said:

My tombstone will be a very large monument where the

public can have access to it. It will be right outside the Metropolitan Opera House, and a fresh supply of red roses will be a prominent sight every day. The monument will become a landmark.

My epitaph will read…Miriam Wolfe was a true performer. She could transport those in the audience to another time and place, if they just believed in her and in themselves. She will remain clear in our memories

Forever.

On January 9, 1989, huddled together at the synagogue cemetery, our two tortured families meet for a private burial. We choose a fitting epitaph for the headstone, and months later, when it is in place, it will read: "She was blissfully talented, full of joy, light and love"—from Ken Bolinsky's letter to Charles Kuralt.

We lay her to rest next to Larry's first wife on a grassy hillside not 100 yards from the original site of the Charter Oak, a historic Annapolis landmark. The cemetery is kitty-corner to Annapolis Mall.

"Maybe this is the right location," I tell Larry. "Miriam loved to shop."

Jewish tradition has it that you place a pebble on the grave you've come to visit. A few months later at Miriam's grave, Larry and I discover an eighteen-inch-tall stuffed Snoopy, dressed in corduroy railroad overalls. Sure enough, in the front pocket, we find a large pebble. I remember Ken Bolinsky's poignant reference to Miriam as a "pebble in a pocket." What a concept.

The stalwart Snoopy keeping Miriam company brings me to tears. But we have no idea who left him, so we carry him home to cherish and shelter him from the elements. Many months later, I coax a confession from a modest Tara Unger— a gifted writer and high school friend of Miriam's who has visited her grave often, leaving poems, stuffed animals, and messages conveying her intense feelings.

A few weeks later, the following letter, written by Tara, appears at the grave. Her eloquence says it all.

Dear Mr. Murderer:

I just wanted to drop you a line and see how you were doing. How are your children? Do you listen adoringly as they chime about their day at school, or about how much they love you? My friend's mother will never again hear the sweet, excited voice telling her of the triumphs and joys in life. And your wife? Does she bring you all the joy and love my friend never had a chance to give? Mr. Murderer, let me tell you—she was full of love, light and joy. She touched everyone she met, giving them a special gift that few have been chosen to give. And when your children cry at night? Do you hold them in your arms? Does your charming way soothe their fears, ease the tender hearts? No one comforted my friend seconds before your filthy bomb took her from this world. From those who loved her. From those she would have loved. And when her broken body met the earth, were you dancing with your soulmate? To her most loved song? Were your children asleep in their beds? Far removed from horrors? From barbarism? When they look into your eyes, do they see the fire? The death? When your little girl slips from your lap is there blood on your hands? Does it soak through the delicate lace dress? Does the stench make you ill? Because you are drenched with blood. I could damn you to Hell, or curse your innocent children, Mr. Murderer, but I won't. I condemn you to live a painfully long life—to stare despondency and emptiness in the face, to lie in bed with fear, grief, and loss and to walk hand in hand forever with tragedy and inconsolability. And when you glance over your shoulder each day, may your unspeakable crimes sting your eyes and burn in your ears.

TOP: *Miriam at ages eight months and three years.*
BOTTOM: *Age four; the two of us at*
Hershey Park, Pennsylvania.

ABOVE: *Kindergarten: wearing a crocheted Greek jumper that Grandpa Saul Pollack (my father) brought from one of his international psychoanalytic conventions.*
BELOW: *At age eight, hamming it up with her cousin Marlene Pollack (on right), Grandpa Saul, and his dog Jerome. The girls are wearing tams Grandpa brought from Scotland.*

ABOVE LEFT: *At thirteen, she played basketball, clarinet, and ran the mile.*
ABOVE RIGHT: *Beside her ceramic mask in a community art show. She's saying, through gritted teeth: "Mom, let's get this over with before any of my friends see me."*
BELOW: *Visiting MGM in Los Angeles—on the set of "CHiPs" with actor Robert Pine and her friend Wendy Moser (right).*

ABOVE: *Her first puppy, whom she named Shane Henry.*
BELOW: *Cuddles.*

ABOVE: *Hoppy.*
BELOW: *With our dog Midnight, who was so pitch-black we constantly stumbled over her.*

LEFT: *On vacation with her step-brother, Chris Spencer.*

RIGHT: *Senior year at Severna Park High School, rehearsing with her friend Bonnie for* You Can't Take It with You. *The photo is from* The Capital.

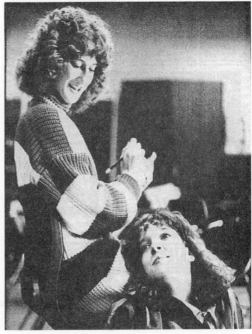

Youth

GREASY KIDSTUFF

Students say play ban is censorship

By JENNIFER TAWES
and MIRIAM WOLFE
Severna Park Senior High

"Grease," the second longest running Broadway musical and blockbuster movie, will not be presented at Severna Park High School this year despite a unanimous vote of the drama club.

The principal of Severna Park High, Oliver Wittig, felt that the play was inappropriate for use in a public school because it advocated "sex, booze and rock 'n' roll."

GUEST WRITERS

These writers are filing a grievance over the play, contending students and parents were inadequately represented on the board that made the decision.

Severna Park High School's Drama Club submitted the musical "Grease" to

MIRIAM WOLFE
Drama Club President

JENNIFER TAWES
Drama Club member

Photos by J. Henson

should be permitted to produce "One Flew Over The Cuckoo's Nest."

The state board's decision was made with the hope that "the immediate issue presented in this appeal will hopefully not recur."

Wittig's decision to reject "Grease" is in opposition to the state Board of Education's call for consistency. This lack of consistency within the county is easily remedied.

One former Severna Park MOI committee member offered the solution that "the county should be consistent in its bylaws, while still maintaining MOI committees in each school." The school's MOI function would then be to alter, if necessary, the objectionable scenes to suit the community's standards.

Moreover, the MOI committee should operate by holding meetings at which oral arguments are presented, rather than simply submitting individual opinions without any discussion. The MOI committee should not have to continue

ABOVE: *Severna Park High graduation photos, two views.*
BELOW: *My three girls, May 1987. With me, from left: Jackie*
Mild Lau, Myrna Mild Spurrier (receiving her master's in art
education), and Miriam.

ABOVE: *Syracuse University, sophomore year—the two of us in her dorm room.* BELOW: *The way we were. With Larry (her new stepdad), Grandpa Saul, and me.*

Performing, sophomore year, in the Syracuse University Drama Department.

ABOVE LEFT: *Makeup magic.*

ABOVE RIGHT: *"Vamping" it up to sing in the Drama Department's holiday cabaret.*

RIGHT: *As the shrill, fluttery Mrs. Spencer in* Anne of Green Gables.

"London is exciting, expensive, and endearing," she wrote in September of her junior year.
ABOVE: *At a London cafe with three friends—her roommate, Jessica Frankel (lower left), Christine Venier, and Anne Husak (middle).*
BELOW: *In Amsterdam.*

ABOVE: *On a three-day trip to Wales.*
RIGHT: *Her grave in Annapolis, Maryland.*

We remember them: The memorial wall at Syracuse University.

ABOVE: *The Garden of Remembrance in Lockerbie, Scotland.*
BELOW: *Arlington National Cemetery. There the memorial is a
Scottish cairn—270 stones, one for each victim, mined from a
quarry near Lockerbie and donated by the Scottish people.*

CHAPTER SEVEN

The Room Where She Lives

IT WILL always be Miriam's room, a room full of irrefutable evidence that she once lived, loved and made a difference on this earth. The decor she selected still delights me: lime green and lemon yellow, and one wall of wild rabbits romping in daisies. Seven-foot-tall bookcases overflow with books and *tchotchkes*—music boxes, candles, china animals. Art prints grace the walls—Renoir's *Luncheon of the Boating Party*, Picasso's *Don Quixote*, and an Andrew Wyeth *Helga* portrait. The desk is stuffed with letters, postcards, and birthday cards, too treasured to throw away. I find photographs—in albums, tucked into drawers and slipped between surprise pages anywhere. For me Miriam lives here. The experience is far from gloomy or unnatural or excessive—rather, it is inspirational.

Sitting down at her desk, I open a leather photo album to a fading shot of a clapboard Cape Cod with wraparound porch, the house where Miriam was born.

My first husband, Jim Wolfe, and I relocated to this College Park, Maryland, house when he took a position with the federal government. The move from New York City cost me my job as an assistant editor at *Harper's* magazine, and at age thirty-two, I found myself applying for the role of motherhood.

On September 26, 1968, six-pound two-ounce Miriam burst into our world. She arrived twelve days early, already in a hurry. Her arrival characterized the way she lived every day of her twenty years: rushing, impatient to fit it all in. We spent the rest of her life running behind her trying to catch up.

The moment she was placed in my arms, I anxiously gave her the once-over: a mat of light brown hair, scrunched up little face, perfect tiny fingers and toes. Oh, and a large nose, but that was okay—so was mine. Miriam's unquenchable appetite arrived almost immediately, but her tense, career-focused mom just didn't fit the earth mother image. Good-bye, breast-feeding. Hello, Similac.

Baby pictures. A steel bar connects her baby shoes. At two months her feet were noticeably pigeon-toed. The pediatrician prescribed the special shoes, forcing her feet outward. Laced into the shoes for the first time, she howled in protest—but not for long. She began entertaining herself by lying on her back, raising her tiny thin legs like a weight-lifter, pumping iron at three months. Soon she was flipping over, hopping about the house like a bunny. At six months the special shoes came off. Still she continued to hop on both knees. I had read that crawling was an essential stage in learning to read, so I got down on the floor and pushed her knees one after the other. In a few minutes she got the idea.

Our new home in Severna Park, Maryland—a four-bedroom colonial, white with red brick. The neighborhood teemed with toddlers and Jim liked being near the water—between two scenic tributaries of the Chesapeake Bay just eight miles north of historic Annapolis.

As I pushed the stroller down Kennedy Drive, I began to revel in the luxury of full-time motherhood. Miriam was turning out to be the most interesting person I'd ever met. At 2-1/2, she started developing an uncanny intuition. Early one morning she studied her father as he rushed out to the car, facing a new job with a long commute. Sensing his anxiety, she called to him from the front door: "Daddy, get along with people!"

Page after page of toddler photos in our fenced backyard. Shortly after sending her out to play, I heard a gentle knock at the back door. I didn't respond soon enough—a much louder, more desperate knock followed. "Mommy, let me in. It's Miriam, your child."

Miriam stands teary-eyed in a doorway with her nursery school teacher, waving good-bye...her first day. Weeks later, I learned that she'd been crying every day.

"Do you let Miriam dress herself?" her teacher asked at our first conference. Confused, I shook my head. "Let her," the teacher urged. "It'll help her become more independent."

The next day Miriam chose her own clothes. I gritted my teeth as I dropped her off in her misbuttoned red jacket, pink suede oxfords and red tights sans skirt. On a field trip with her class three weeks later, the teacher reported to me: "We just love the way Miriam dresses herself. We can't wait to see what she'll wear next." The tactic worked; her crying stopped, her confidence grew, and in time, her outfits even matched.

As much as I loved motherhood, I missed my career. I found a compromise, a copy-editing position with a large medical and scientific publisher in Baltimore. Best of all, I could work at home. I brought Miriam to the office with me to deliver a completed assignment. Fifty women copy editors and only a couple men bent over their desks. My three-year-old sized the place up:

"There are too many ladies here," she said. You got that right, Miriam.

Miriam at age eight sitting up in a hospital bed. Sitting up indeed. She had been sedated prior to surgery to remove a cyst from her cheek—evidently not sedated well enough. She rode the gurney down the hall to the OR bolt upright, waving to nurses and other patients.

"What are you doing up?" the astonished oral surgeon asked. Just my daughter not wanting to miss anything.

Miriam engrossed in her newest stack of library books.... So often she reminded me of those Early American primitive paintings that portrayed small children as miniature grown-ups. She seemed to have been born with an adult sense of purpose. She inherited this trait from my mother, a journalist and author, who fought through decades of illness to accomplish a lifetime in forty-eight years. "Do it now while it's fresh," she often admonished my brother and me. This sense of urgency propelled Miriam too; the intensity infused her whole life.

I replace the first volume on the shelf and my eyes fix on a jar filled with fifty sharks' teeth. Miriam and I had gathered the teeth on our family vacation to the Outer Banks of North Carolina; she collected others from Chesapeake Beach in Maryland. A kindly paleontologist at the Smithsonian in Washington identified them for us and Miriam assembled them into a first-grade school science fair project. In succeeding years, the science fairs awarded her prizes for "A Trip Through a Cow's Stomach"; "How a Telephone Works"; "Turning Rocks Into Jewelry"; and in sixth grade, "How Alcohol Affects the Body," which netted her a countywide third place, a gold medal, and a $25 check.

She sprawls on the floor amid her Barbies. On a summer day in her eighth year, Miriam emptied the small suitcase that held her Barbie clothes, filled it with a few of her own and started down the stairs. Encountering me in the front hall, she stopped and declared, "I'm running away. Talk me out of it."

I did. But then I took her in my arms and asked her why she wanted to run away. Tears flooded her azure blue eyes and she hid her curly blond head in my chest.

"Because you and Daddy argue so much," she whispered.

A shot of the three of us in front of the house. No one is smiling. Even the absence of smiles couldn't reveal the extent of the turmoil overtaking our little family. After two decades as an editor, I bolted from my introverted profession and became a real estate agent. But I'd never worked on straight commission before. How did anyone pay the mortgage in this business?

I had to learn fast. My husband and I lived in a boating paradise and owned two sailboats, but there were no calm waters at our house. Our marriage was headed for the rocks. Perhaps it was inevitable. We had gravitated to each other as complete opposites, but the charm eventually wore off. On New Year's Eve, 1977, while the rest of the world sipped champagne, Jim and I bitterly slammed doors and shouted our angry good-byes. Good-bye to seventeen years of marriage.

As I return this pain-filled album to its place, my eye catches a title on the shelf above. Shortly after Miriam died, I discovered a yellow scrap of paper among her college notebooks. On it she'd written: "Show Mom p. 60 of *The Road Less Traveled.*" Trembling, I opened the book. Page 60 criticized parents who think they're protecting their children by hiding the truth:

"Such protection is unsuccessful. The children know anyway that Mommy and Daddy had a fight the night before.... The result then is not protection but deprivation.... [The children] are deprived of role models of openness and honesty."

Miriam was nine when her father and I separated. She and I got to keep the house—her life's continuity being foremost in all our minds. We spent many tearful hours talking about divorce, but mostly she cried and begged, "You can get back together, if you only try." She made up a game to act out the reconciliation: Barbie and Ken Get Married. Her frustration turned confrontational, I yelled a lot, and we entered the year of living disastrously.

A photo of Miriam on her knees in the living room, hugging her dog. I take a deep breath and run my tongue over my lips. Within six months of my separation, all six of our pets—Shane (the dog), Cuddles (the kitten), Teeny and Tiny (the two gerbils), and two anonymous goldfish—ascended to pet heaven. Had I put a hex on them? No, but perhaps our misery infected them and they all just decided to call it quits.

No matter how justified I felt when our marriage ended, I still felt an equal measure of guilt. I asked myself over and over whether things could have been different. I dredged up specific fragments of our conflicts and reconstructed them in my mind. If I'd done this or that, maybe... And as I careened from one task to another through those early days, I discovered that earning a living, raising a child, and running a house was a high-wire act, but one that I was determined to master—or else.

Miriam's anguish wrenched me. We both needed help and I turned to my psychoanalyst father, who provided us with moral support, excellent books about coping with divorce, and a generous measure of financial assistance as well. At moments when I dwelt on my own plight he reminded me, on the phone from Milwaukee, to think of my child first: "We know what you need, but what does Miriam need?"

I began seeing a local psychiatrist once a week and took Miriam for her own visits too. The therapy gave me the courage and self-confidence to carve out my new life as a single mother.

Years later, Miriam admitted to me: "I hated your marriage." And therein lay the ambivalence for us both. We found it so hard to face up to the end of the dream—the stereotype of the happy family. But the conflicts in our home had been so intense that within weeks of my separation, relatives and friends told me: "You and Miriam are so much more relaxed now."

Shots of Miriam as she played with her brand-new kitten. I rewarded her for making the honor role. Another pet— would I never learn? He sat poised atop an end table in our living room. With his glowing yellow eyes and Buddha posture, he looked like the last accessory the decorator had set down. Hoppy mastered kitchen cabinet and refrigerator doors. No Froot Loops box escaped his raids. When he got bellyaches, Miriam tried to spoon-feed him Pepto-Bismol, which he firmly declined, of course. So she dribbled it across his paws and he frantically licked them clean. Success!

A picture of Miriam and me, a stack of Multiple Listing printouts under my arm. Two-and-a-half years of selling houses, and the roller-coaster income, just about did me in. The final straw: I discovered there was no such thing as a reliable

baby-sitter who was also a wallflower and always available eve-
nings and weekends. Even taking Miriam along on my ap-
pointments didn't work. She tried to be helpful. But not all
buyers were charmed by my ten-year-old running up the stairs
ahead of us, calling out: "Wait till you see the master bed-
room!"

I returned to the Baltimore publishing house to edit medical books and journals. This time I put in twenty-one hours in
the office to get benefits and twenty more at home to raise my
daughter in peace and good conscience.

*Five laughing little girls waving from the windows of my
Chevy Chevette. Carpool time.* My new life could have been
solitary and self-pitying. But not with Miriam for a daughter.
She did something for me that nobody else could have done:
she brought purpose and a sense of community to my world. I
always found a reason to be somewhere, to be doing something—helping with homework or class projects, getting her to
religious school, the library, Girl Scouts, and softball. I became
fast friends with some of her friends' parents. Yeah, I car-
pooled my brains out. And sometimes I went overboard playing supermom. But being Miriam's mother enriched my life.

And Miriam actually had big plans for me. She wrote a letter to Howard Keel, my favorite actor on *Dallas*, inviting him
to our house for a drink—and signed my name. I wasn't dating
and she thought I needed a little boost. (I intercepted the letter. Hey, maybe I shouldn't have.)

Miriam and her friend Shannon playing dress-up. Shannon's mother referred to her daughter as "My Shannon," and I
liked that, so I spoke of Miriam to a friend on the phone in
the same way. She overheard me.

"I am not your Miriam," she retorted. "I'm eleven years
old and I don't belong to anyone. I'm my own person."
Oooookay, I couldn't dispute her logic.

I had often felt my marital identity depended on my lob-
ster Cantonese and veal scaloppini. After the divorce, I retired
from gourmet cooking—big time.

"Mom?" Miriam asked timidly one night, "Do you think we could have something for dinner that doesn't come in a box?"

But when I did make the effort, I'd chop, chop, chop to create an overflowing platter of the tacos she loved—and she'd eat one. "It's delicious, Mom, but I'm full." She ate six bird-like meals a day, never gained any weight, never went over 112 pounds; her rocketlike energy just burned it away.

A Chanukah card—a paper menorah she made for me at age twelve, with this message written between the candles:

"Mom—I don't like myself when I'm selfish, but I can't help it. I'm glad it snowed today so that your flight will be delayed. Sorry. I'll miss you."

Miriam wasn't the only one with misgivings. In December 1980 I was packing for my first convention as the new managing editor of *Chemical Times & Trends,* the journal of the Chemical Specialties Manufacturers Association. I was so nervous I secretly hoped for a blizzard to keep me from getting to Miami Beach. But my trip proved a great success, and when I returned I got an earful from Miriam of her own adventures. She had written a fan letter to Dear Abby and a letter to President Jimmy Carter advising him on how to clean up the environment.

Now here's a shot of Miriam in the kitchen with the telephone at her ear. How natural it looks—as though it were an extension of her anatomy.

In junior high, two major influences dominated her life: the telephone and *General Hospital.* At 9:30 one evening I returned home from a meeting and found our sitter greeting me, ashen-faced. Miriam was calling MGM in Hollywood, trying to reach her favorite *GH* actress. "Get off the phone this minute!" I yelled.

And every week we watched the TV show *Fame.* It planted the seed for a life in the theater. As soon as the theme song came on, Miriam would leap up from the couch to sing and dance along.

"Fame—I'm gonna live forever, I'm gonna learn how to fly."

She'd throw herself into the frenzied jazz beat, her curly hair flopping from side to side. She'd forget her surroundings and become part of the music. At those moments, I too thought she would live forever.

She actually had the opportunity to visit the set of *Fame* in California and mingle with the actors. She darted up to Valerie Lansburg:

"Can I have your autograph?" Miriam asked.

"Sure."

"You're my favorite actress."

"Oh, not me, it should be someone like Glenda Jackson."

"You have a marvelous singing voice, it's beautiful. But you smoke!"

"That's what someone just said to me. I'm grown up. I have a right to smoke."

"Oops, sorry! It was nice meeting you."

"Nice meeting you too."

Miriam holding her clarinet. Piano, clarinet, and the junior high band gave way to voice lessons. Even untrained, her soprano voice had a sweet, vibrant, resonant tone. On her own, at thirteen, she located a professional opera singer/teacher, who accepted her as a student. Four months after beginning the technically demanding voice lessons, she landed her first role—for Children's Theatre of Annapolis. She played the prissy Mrs. Purdy in *Forty-Five Minutes from Broadway*. Thus began several beautiful years with CTA, during which she performed five leading and major roles.

Another playbill: Snow White and the Seven Dwarfs of the Black Forest. Miriam played Queen Bella in that spoof of the fairytale.

"Don't bite the apple," children in the audience screamed at Snow White.

Queen Bella leaned menacingly over the edge of the stage to the littlest ones down front. "Shut up, my dears," she ad-libbed. The children loved it.

But sometimes her nerves got to her. She auditioned for *Brigadoon* at Annapolis Summer Garden Theater. An intimidating setting for a fourteen-year-old: a smoky room filled with experienced adult actors and dancers, and a three-hour wait for her turn. Her warmed-up voice cooled down. The director thought she sang just fine, but she didn't think so. She rushed from the dance line in tears prompted by the difficult choreography. She even refused the resulting "callback"—too embarrassed.

On the third shelf sits John Bartlett's Familiar Quotations—*with at least a dozen of Miriam's Post-its still peeking out of its pages.* I gave her the new edition on her sixteenth birthday. My mother had given me a copy in high school and it was time to pass on the legacy. Miriam embraced it as if she'd been waiting for it her whole life. She bought blank books intended as diaries, and on randomly scattered pages, she copied germaine quotes in calligraphy and gave the books as gifts.

In the one she gave me, the quotes include: "I cannot and will not cut my conscience to fit this year's fashions" (Lillian Hellman); and on the very last page, Daniel Webster's deathbed words "I still live." For the rest of my days I will wonder why she chose that quote.

A CTA playbill for Joseph and the Amazing Technicolor Dreamcoat. After performing the role of co-narrator, she wrote for Honors English:

"I feel an incredible sense of delight. The most delightful feeling I have ever experienced was the sudden rush of applause, and an audience of 700 simultaneously standing. It goes on, and on, and on, and I feel so thrilled I want to burst. A standing ovation and continuous applause are the ultimate forms of approval."

An article from the Arundel Sun *with a photo of Miriam and some of her campers at London Town Publik House.* Now a national museum with rolling lawns and wooded gardens on the South River, it served as a bustling seaport 300 years ago. I had taken an afternoon off to drive her to the job interview, and as I waited in the car, feelings of tenderness and pride almost overwhelmed me. She looked so dignified in her blue suit and white blouse, yet she radiated an innocent charm; and as she slid back into the car, she smiled and announced: "I got the job."

She worked at this Living History camp for three summers, recreating colonial life for children. They made corn husk dolls, studied history and architecture, cooked a pioneer meal on the hearth, wove baskets, dyed cloth from plants. This experience brought her to another great love in her life— teaching.

A *drama club program for Severna Park High's One-Act Play Night.* Miriam entered the competition as a director and chose *Impromptu*, a psychological play. Twenty-five auditioned for the three parts, including one of her close friends. The friend didn't get the part—she wasn't right for it. But Miriam managed to soothe any ruffled feathers and keep the friendship. She also won the award for Best Director and one of her performers won for Best Actress.

Underlying this heady experience lurked the anxiety of choosing a college. She had already chosen her career, musical theater. Was I happy about it? Heavens, no. We discussed the hazards. That is, I harangued. She pirouetted around her room.

You're only as good as your last part, I reminded her. Most actors are unemployed most of the time. The theater attracts, by its very nature, a disproportionate number of petty, clawing, cutthroat, unstable people.

She knew all that. On her vanity sat two framed photos, one of Judy Garland and one of Joan Crawford.

"Dear," I said, trying not to whine, "are these women role models for you? They were so neurotic and had such messed-up lives."

"They were fine artists, Mom," she said, executing an arabesque. "You know, I don't have to become a Mommie Dearest." I had to laugh—but I wasn't quite finished.

"I didn't encourage you to become an actress."

"Oh no? You and Dad had me performing for your friends from the time I was six!"

One of my favorite album pages: a well-researched, polished article in The Capital *entitled "Greasy Kidstuff."* As president of the drama club, Miriam wrote it with her friend Jennifer in a crusade against censorship. Severna Park High refused to let the Spotlighters perform *Grease* because "it contains sex, booze and rock and roll."

"Can you believe it?" Miriam said. "They don't understand that the play's a satire." But the club members did persuade the principal to add a student to the adult committee that made those decisions. Ten years after her crusade, the high school finally performed *Grease.*

Prom night—Miriam in white taffeta with a huge pink satin bow. At sunset on the lawn, the prom couples posed for pictures in *Great Gatsby* splendor. This romantic scene came a day after Miriam begged her date: "Please, please bring your father's car." The week before, she'd gotten trapped in the seat belt of Matt's junker and he'd had to cut her out of it with a scissors.

Her Andrew Wyeth Helga *print catches my eye.* One weekend when my father was visiting, Miriam raced down the stairs to breakfast and burst upon us. "You've got to come with me to see the *Helga* paintings," she said breathlessly. She'd already been to the National Gallery show twice. I was skeptical.

"Won't it be boring, a whole exhibit about just one person?" I asked.

"No," Miriam said, an urgency in her voice. "I want so much to share it with you. You won't be disappointed, I promise." And we weren't. Father, Larry and I were exhilarated. She led us through the rooms like an experienced docent, and later wrote notes of her impressions:

Wyeth's paintings are hypnotizing and endlessly varied.

Helga's plain, sturdy clothes—earnest grays and browns, painted with such exquisite detail you can almost touch the fabric. Sunlight sweeping into a window, ambushing a stark room. Brooding shadows falling on a winter tree. Helga in the fetal position on a bed, with only a bare bulb illuminating her desolate world.

On Senior Awards Night Miriam received the Linda Joy Davies Award for Achievement in the Arts and Humanities, an engraved silver bowl.

Four excellent colleges accepted her, including Syracuse, her first choice, where she had to audition in New York for the Drama Department. Despite accolades and acceptances, Miriam stormed about the house, short tempered and edgy. I assumed it was her anxiety at losing her familiar high school comfort zone to tackle the great unknown ahead. Days later, she confessed, "I was so worried about our two families being together at graduation." Sadly, graduation night Miriam and the Wolfes went for their afterward treat and separately, my father and I went for ours. How ironic that since her death we have all gotten along just fine.

Miriam in front of her dorm—trying hard to look cheerful—on her eighteenth birthday. Her birthday fell on the Friday of Parents Weekend and I eagerly flew up. What a disaster. She cried the whole weekend. The school had squeezed her and two roommates into a room so tiny they couldn't even use one of the desks; they had to stack it on top of another one just to be able to walk around. I had brought a birthday cake sporting yellow roses, but where to set it down? I had to hold it on my lap. The dorm reminded me of Animal House. Thundering humanity, no privacy, no way to quietly study or practice voice lessons. Heavy drinking. "You can't even go into the bathroom on weekends, Mom, everybody's throwing up."

And the intensity of the Drama Department took some getting used to. When she wasn't doing research for the production of *Hamlet,* she was mopping the stage till midnight.

She learned the craft of lighting the hard way. "I pulled the wrong lever and the whole stage went dark. It wasn't funny, Mom."

She wrote to a high school teacher:

> For the most part, I'm happy. The Drama Department is full of talented, dedicated people. But because all of the actor's work is based on self, it's easy to lose our perspective as to who we really are. I always thought I had a good sense of self, but now I'm not so sure. I only know that I'm a very different person from when I left.

A photo of Miriam sitting on our front porch, radiant in a fuchsia turtleneck and jeans. She wrote in her journal about coming home for Thanksgiving:

> As the station wagon swings past the entrance to my community, my heart beats in anticipation. The maple tree that brushes its leaves against my bedroom window is the first thing framed in the car window. I am home at last. As I squint, I recognize that orange and white lump in the middle of the yard. My cat yawns, as if to say, "I'm glad you're home, but I'm too proud to show it."
>
> Now the car is pulling into the driveway and I open the door before it stops rolling. I sprint across the yard, take the front porch steps all in one leap, and run smack into my mother. She and I giggle and hug each other as my dog runs in circles around us. Midnight greets me with a kiss and I stroke her soft fur. A feeling of warmth envelops me, and suddenly my life is in perspective again. I am safe, warm, and loved.

That night I introduced my daughter to my new boyfriend, Larry, and he listened with attention and amazement while she talked his ear off for four straight hours.

"Larry is really romantic," I told Miriam as we were getting ready for bed that night. "What do you think of him?"

"I think you should marry him," she promptly answered.

By the end of her freshman year, Larry and I were engaged and we drove up to Syracuse to bring her home. We found her with only half a suitcase packed amid a Mount Everest of clothes, books, tapes, stereo speakers, and makeup.

"Miriam," I said, "we need a Roadway semi." And was she testy with us. We were interfering with her good-byes to her friends. In a pounding rain, Larry tied down the open trunk lid with rope—no way could we close it—and scotch-taped plastic trash liners around the Honda's hindside. We stuffed Miriam into the few empty inches of the back seat for the seven-hour drive home in the nonstop downpour without benefit of rearview mirror.

Another photo—my new Toyota Corolla. I bought my car to celebrate my new job as an engineering writer for Westinghouse. It meant a higher salary, better benefits, and a shorter commute, but lots of overtime. Now there was less of me available for both Miriam and Larry. She, of course, was having a tough time adjusting to us; she'd had her mother all to herself for nine years. While packing up his own house to move into mine just before the wedding, Larry spent several nights a week at our house. One night when we'd retired early, Miriam, in a mischievous mood, put the sensual Ravel's *Bolero* on the stereo and turned the volume up to deafening. I felt like I was living the movie *Ten.* Assuming she'd done it for our benefit, we ignored her. But I was mortified.

Part of her pain in feeling she was losing something of her mother was her yearning to have a serious boyfriend of her own. In a letter to a close friend, she wrote: "Mom and Larry are sickeningly cute together and in love. How I envy them." Many men were interested in her, but a real relationship hadn't gelled yet. In her journal freshman year, she wrote about the young man she was dating at SU. "He's so possessive—and we haven't even gotten to know each other yet. He wants to *have* a girlfriend. He wants her to belong to him, whereas I want to be *with* someone, to enjoy and appreciate each other."

Larry and I were married at Temple Beth Shalom on Thanksgiving weekend of Miriam's sophomore year. We came out of the rabbi's study and stood at the back. Miriam, seated next to my father in the front row, stood and faced us, and sang "Unexpected Song" from Andrew Lloyd Webber's *Song and Dance*. In her vibrant voice, so fresh and bell-like, she sang just to us and for us. The song begins:

> *I have never felt like this,*
> *for once I'm lost for words,*
> *your smile has really thrown me.*
> *This is not like me at all,*
> *I never thought I'd know*
> *the kind of love you've shown me.*
> *Now no matter where I am,*
> *no matter what I do,*
> *I see your face appearing.*
> *Like an unexpected song,*
> *an unexpected song that only we are hearing.*

On that day Miriam acquired her two stepsisters. And because both are gifted artists (as well as teachers)—Jackie a sculptor and Myrna a ceramist—the three new sisters forged an immediate bond that reached beyond love to creativity.

After a lunch during winter break with her three best friends from high school, Miriam wrote in her journal:

> It was so nice to know that, despite the fact that our lives are different now, we can still relate to one another. I've never felt better than I did at that luncheon—so secure, so peaceful, so at ease with being me. It's a good thing, too, because the Drama Department was beginning to make me wonder. At Bay Country theater camp I was

taught: "Always be sincere in your own life. There are lots of artificial actressy types and they get in trouble because they don't know what's real any more. If you feel insecure, be insecure, etc." At home, I'm real, I've earned the right to be real. At school the same thing must happen.

By the end of freshman year she felt at home at college too. *I find a playbill from SU's production of* Anne of Green Gables. The *Syracuse Post-Standard* said: "Wonderfully fresh and entertaining.... Fine characterizations. Miriam Wolfe played Mrs. Spencer as a muddled Mrs. Malaprop with a shrill voice and fluttering mannerisms."

Larry and I drove up to Syracuse to see her in the play *Woyzeck*, an allegory of mob psychology. A fellow cast member gave her a note before opening night: "You are a very intelligent, incredible human being. Don't be so hard on yourself!"

In a term paper on the French Impressionist painter Berthe Morisot, Miriam wrote: "She drove herself relentlessly, her expectations were uncompromisingly high." My daughter could just as easily have been describing herself.

A playbill of Woody Allen's Don't Drink the Water *for the Pasadena (Maryland) Theatre Company.* In June after her sophomore year, she won the role of the ingenue Susan Hollander. The male lead, a seasoned actor twice her age, wrote her a note:

"...By observing the way you 'slide into' a character: experimenting, choosing role models, changing attitudes and inflections; and by watching you on stage whenever possible: movements, gestures, poses, etc.—from these observations I have been able to apply many new ideas to my own character and to my acting in general. It has really helped. For that I want to thank you."

When she wasn't on stage, she had more personal preoccupations. In her journal, she wrote:

Don't Drink the Water opened tonight and I feel I gave a

good solid performance. Now that I have to do love
scenes, that's one hurdle I'm over. I just wish that the
only heavy-duty kissing I've ever been involved with
wasn't because I'm in a show. All I know is I want to get
over this preoccupation with my sexuality. I want to lose
my virginity! There, I've said it! I feel like half a woman, a
mutant. But it's got to be with the right guy.

...My date last night with David was wonderful. The
Annapolis Brass Quintet played beautifully. At the Chart
House we chatted over tea and mud pies and then drove
back to his house. We talked from eleven o'clock on.
Finally he put his arm around me. So we ended up lying
on the couch the entire night. (Talk about taking a risk!)
It was so nice; someone twenty-three, attractive, intelligent, who finds me both his intellectual equal and physi-
cally attractive. How nice to lie there while he stroked my
hair and back and just *talk*! Things like this always happen
when you don't look for them. Too bad he lives so far
away now. I didn't want a long distance relationship, but
it looks like I've no choice. Well, there certainly are worse
things!

At home before leaving for her summer job, she sang in a
friend's wedding and donated her 300 stuffed animals to the
YWCA battered spouse shelter.

One afternoon as I came in from work, I heard a tearful
voice calling to me from the kitchen.

"Mom," Miriam wailed, "I had an accident in the Naval
Academy parking lot. I hit a Mercedes! The midshipman said
it was a graduation present from his dad." Then she cheered
herself up. "At least it was a used Mercedes," she said.

The bright-red scrapbook from Darien Lake. Miriam auditioned for and landed a summer job singing and dancing at
Darien Lake, the largest theme park in New York state. Three
days after she got there, she wrote to her friend Jessica:

"...I have to learn twenty-four songs and the choreography in six days. I don't know if I can do it. I'm on an emotional roller coaster. Today I burst into tears out of frustration. But every time I get discouraged, I think of what you told me—how good this'll be for me and how it'll cure my stage fright. I have five numbers where I dance with someone from the audience. When I first started learning the choreography for 'Material Girl,' I thought: This is sexy stuff—they must be thinking of someone else! But I'm getting it!"

A photo of Miriam and me at Darien Lake. I visited her for a long weekend to celebrate my birthday, while Larry was in England on business, and she showered me with surprises. A Happy Birthday banner. Two pairs of earrings, three jars of strawberry jam she had made, cheese, crackers and fruit, all carefully wrapped in a straw basket. That night she stayed with me at the Holiday Inn and we talked till 3 A.M. The next day I learned what it was like to be totally immersed in show biz.

"Backstage" was a tiny cubbyhole and the routines were grueling. But they were also delightful. I sat through six shows and loved every minute. Miriam and two other singers, plus a lively backup band comprised "The Heart of Rock 'n' Roll," with songs from the '50s to the '80s. And sure enough, by performing thirty-two shows a week, she got over her stage fright.

"What do you do between shows?" I asked her.

"Sometimes we color," she said, pointing to her large pile of coloring books and crayons. Which didn't surprise me. At Syracuse she'd bought herself a Mr. Potato Head.

During my visit, we sat at a picnic table and talked—at one point, about my divorce.

"I don't think I started growing up until I got divorced," I told her.

She looked at me, astonished. "Then we grew up together," she said.

A photo of Miriam standing next to her father. A three-pack-a-day smoker, he had just quit, on doctor's orders. Miriam had been begging him to quit for years. In high school she had bombarded him with literature she'd ordered from the American Lung Association.

Nestled among the albums is the journal Miriam kept that summer at Darien Lake. The entry for June 20:

> Now I'm sitting on the grass, next to the water ski show and behind the ferris wheel. There are gulls here—they remind me of home. So does the smell by the ferris wheel—exactly like Market House chicken. It brings back a flood of memories of the City Dock in Annapolis. Dad and me at the Market House—regardless of the season or weather. Potatoes and chicken, wrapped in tinfoil...paper bags...napkins...walking arm in arm eating on the tiny ledge and staring out at the bleakness of the bay in winter. Only locals to look at—old men—fishermen, with caps, flannel shirts, and jackets. Summer—chocolate ice cream from a sugar cone, dripping. Tourists in matching red, white, and blue outfits. Colorful, preppy Annapolis. Main Street, the old bookshop, where Dad buys me three new books.
>
> And walking on the rocks at the Naval Academy— extra fast—I'm good at this. Scan and step, scan and step quicker. The sea wall, wind whipping my hair back, feet on a slippery rock, waves splashing my feet. Extra splashes—the wake from the Harbor Queen. Wave to the tourists. They wave back, smiling. I wave to the boaters on the Severn River. Those in day-sailers—wish I were one of them. Or the Egg Harbor owners, with their Formica tables with dried flowers arranged in a vase; the living room of their vessel looks more like a house. Not salty at all! But look at this British racing green hull, a double-ender. There's a mahogany hull—two nut-brown sails, gaff-rigged, running, beautiful—look at the upkeep on the wood. Wow! God, I miss those times.

A photo of Miriam, Myrna, and Jackie, arm in arm, laughing.

Miriam returned home from Darien Lake jubilant from her success and new friendships, especially with a young man named Jake. We had only three days to pack her for London. Only three days to be together.

Myrna and Tim spent Miriam's last evening with us. Myrna was seven months pregnant with their first child. As they were leaving for home, Miriam said: "Wait a minute."

She raced up the stairs and back down again. Cradling a three-foot-tall teddy bear, she held it out to Myrna. "I want you to have this," she said. Her sister reached out her arms for it. Today the bear sits on Craig's bed in Kamuela, Hawaii, its fur flattened from two generations of hugs.

At ten o'clock that night, both of us totally worn out, Miriam and I finished the packing. She pulled a garment bag out of the closet.

"I haven't had a chance to model my new coat for you," she said. "Jake helped me pick it out in Buffalo." As she slid her arms into the sleeves, she was suddenly transformed into a brilliant burst of fire-engine red. She whirled around, striking a high-fashion runway pose.

"Jake told me I have beautiful legs," she said, laughing. She threw her arms around me and laid her head on my shoulder.

CHAPTER EIGHT

Unexpected Gifts

HOW IS it possible for any personal belongings to survive an explosion at 31,000 feet—nearly six miles high? And even if they did, how could they survive intact, lying for days, even weeks, in the countryside exposed to the bitter Scottish winter? But they did. And because of the compassion and goodness of the people of Lockerbie, most of the Pan Am Flight 103 families have gotten back at least a few of their loved one's belongings.

Lockerbie police and volunteers painstakingly combed an 845-square-mile area and retrieved almost 18,000 items—clothes, cameras, film, wrapped holiday gifts, souvenirs, even whole suitcases. The Lockerbie community built a warehouse, where they inventoried and catalogued every item, even down to a single coat sleeve. They installed washing machines and dryers. Volunteer women of Lockerbie washed and ironed every piece of clothing, every item in every mildewed suitcase, every pathetic scattered fragment. They carefully dried soggy diaries, letters, passports, wallets, school notebooks, and term papers. They even ironed the pages of journals to keep them intact. Every item was returned to the families—carefully, lovingly wrapped in tissue paper, resealable plastic bags, and neat boxes. The Scottish police kept rolls of undeveloped film until they had finished their criminal investigation. They returned Miriam's film to me—in packages of developed large prints.

Nine years and nine months after Miriam's death, Larry and I visited Lockerbie for the first time. My brother and sister-in-law, John and Ann Pollack, gave us much-needed moral support. At the Town Hall, Janet Anderson guided us to memorabilia of Flight 103, including a magnificent stained glass window of twenty-one flags representing the victims' homelands. There we also met Mr. Bogie, a regional official of southwest Scotland.

Donald T. Bogie, M.B.E. (Member of the British Empire), received this title from Queen Elizabeth for his leadership and dedication in the recovery of remains and personal effects in the Flight 103 tragedy. He's also in charge of the cemetery where the Garden of Remembrance memorial resides. We had made prior arrangements with him to install a bronze plaque for Miriam. It sits at the base of a teardrop-shaped bed of dazzling purple and red flowers—as if Miriam were welcoming visitors. We expressed our thanks to Peter Rae, the stonemason, who had driven 200 miles that very morning to install the plaque before our arrival. Donald then drove us to a lovely small garden at the end of a lane honoring the eleven Lockerbie residents who also lost their lives.

And finally, he took us to Tundergarth, three miles from town. A tiny stone chapel—a serene setting for contemplation—contains a book inscribed with each victim's name. A mile away, on the rolling green fields where sheep peacefully graze, he pointed to the spot where Miriam was found.

We had arrived in Lockerbie with enormous trepidation. We came away feeling uplifted. We were awed by the sensitivity, exquisite taste, and tenderness of this remarkable community. Their love and kindness still rise to overcome the evil that befell us all.

If Pam Am 103 had exploded just ten minutes later, it would have been over the Atlantic Ocean in such deep water that all would have been lost forever—the plane, the passengers, their personal effects. It also would have meant that any investigation of the cause of the explosion would have been impossible. I had no concept of the difficulties investigators would face in even a hundred feet of water until the explosion of TWA Flight 800 over Long Island Sound in July 1996.

A funny thing how, overnight, your priorities can shift. On the morning of December 21, my main worry was that Miriam would miss her connection to BWI and have to spend the night at JFK. From the next day on, my deepest anxiety, my obsession was to get her body returned home to us. Now Larry and I feel "fortunate" (how ironic to even use the word) that we were able to bury her in our family plot only eight miles from our home. Seventeen Pan Am families are not so lucky; their loved ones will never be recovered, just because of where they had the misfortune to sit in the plane.

My second obsession is to get her personal effects back— if there are any. Somehow, it never occurs to me that there won't be. The first week in February 1989, the Consulate General of the United States in Edinburgh sends me an affidavit to fill in and get notarized that I am the next of kin, entitled to receive Miriam's things. The Consulate General also asks me to send them a list describing everything Miriam had with her. Sure. This is something concrete I can do to help. I whip out a yellow legal pad and pen. But the more I try to recall everything she and I jammed into her suitcases, the more my memory falls short. And of course she bought many things overseas.

Help comes from her friend Heather. Over a tearful supper at a restaurant in Annapolis, she describes the textbooks they bought for their classes in London, the clothes Miriam wore, her jewelry. I gratefully write it all down on my pad. Then Heather digs deep into her purse and pulls out a blank book with a shiny gray cover.

"Miriam got one of these to use as a journal," she says. "I liked it so much I decided to buy one for myself." I finger its smoothness, turn it over and over, and add it to my list.

Back home, too agitated to sleep even at 2 A.M., I sit down at the computer and compile my list for the Consulate General. The next day I mail it, along with the notarized affidavit. Soon after, I receive the first "inventory of personal effects."

At the top of the page it says "...Estate of Miriam Luby Wolfe Found Dead on December 24, 1988." I suppose it's a legal matter, but why, oh, why does it have to remind me? I already know it, I've been subjected to it on the death certificate. Three lonesome items are listed and do I want them? Yes, of course, I immediately write back.

Two months after Pan Am 103 exploded, I receive the first of four packages of Miriam's personal belongings—that is, the first of her belongings that the Scottish police were able to recover.

Crying, my hands shaking as I open the tiny package, I can only think, This isn't real, this isn't happening to me. Inside I find one earring, a watch, and only the metal loop from the other earring. Miriam was wearing them on the plane home. The silver earring is one of a pair she had received for Chanukah—tiny tragedy and comedy masks. My God! It's the lone *tragedy* mask that stares up at me so heartbreakingly, so eerily from its plastic wrapper.

And the watch—a gift from my father on Miriam's twentieth birthday—it's still running! I can't bear to even look at it. I tuck it away in a drawer.

On May 7, 1989, I receive the second package, a huge box. I leave work early to pick it up at the post office. It's so heavy the postmaster carries it to my car. He has a somber look on his face—he's seen the return address.

I wait anxiously for Larry to get home from work. He carries the box from the car upstairs to Miriam's room—that's where I'd like to open it. And I want him with me—I don't want to open it alone.

Inside the cardboard container sits my maroon soft-sided suitcase, the smaller of the two I had lent Miriam to take to London. It smells musty and the frame is dented. But inside, meticulously wrapped, are her clothes: dresses, pants, socks, sweaters, swim suit, tights and underwear, her shoes, her purses. Everything washed, ironed, folded neatly, and wrapped in plastic bags. Many of the clothes are still in excellent, wearable condition. Surviving an explosion six miles high in the sky? It's unfathomable.

I start crying and can't stop. As I lift each item out, I remember where we bought it and what she looked like wearing it. The red umbrella I had bought only two days before she left for London to match her new red coat. The little red Kodak camera I gave her as an advance birthday present—cracked beyond repair. The trendy denim jacket she wore all spring at Syracuse. The pink raincoat my father bought her in Milwaukee on her last trip there. Some of the clothes, though cleaned so carefully and lovingly by the women of Lockerbie, are covered with mildew, irreparably damaged. Those that are salvageable I'll donate to charity.

I discover a fragile silver angel meant for the top of a Christmas tree. It's in almost perfect condition. A Frisbee from the Hard Rock Cafe in Amsterdam. A fat paperback of the British Museum filled with color photos. A navy blue Oxford University sweatshirt.

A month from now, her roommate will visit us. We'll sit on the floor of Miriam's room and silently go through the box together. She'll recognize everything. These are gifts: the angel for Miriam's stepmother, the Frisbee for Chris, the book for Larry. The weekend before Miriam left for London, Larry had shown her his scrapbook of his recent business trip there—he raved about the British Museum. How like Miriam to choose a gift so personal, just for him.

Delving deeper into the box, I discover a packet of beautiful art cards on which Miriam had written holiday notes, but not yet mailed them. I'll mail them for her. Friends and relatives have already been informing me, reluctantly, afraid to upset me, that they've received notes from Miriam a day or two after her death. At my request, they send me copies or the notes themselves. Jim's mother and Miriam corresponded from the time Miriam was seven. Grandma Bert sends me all seventy-five of her letters and cards.

Through my tears I see a black book bag and another large

carry-on, both crammed with books, notebooks, and sheet music. They have crushed corners and a mildewed smell, but they're all still readable.

And then I discover Miriam's journal. I call it the Pooh Journal. It's a small lined notebook, the size and shape of an exam blue book. On the cover is an illustration of Winnie-the-Pooh and Piglet holding hands, walking through the forest with a caption: "It's so much friendlier with two."

Lying in the suitcase in the Scottish countryside, the journal of course become wet and muddy. The first ten pages, although now dry, are almost illegible. The ink has faded almost to nothingness. For the next two weeks on my lunch hours, I set the journal on my artist's light table at work as I decipher the faded ten pages. Here is an excerpt from the Pooh Journal:

10/30…Yesterday Christine and I left the roar of the city behind and set out for Wales—on a train to Carmarthen. We shuffled out of the station, bags in hand, and observed the landscape, which sharply asserted itself against the cold cobalt sky. To our left, a stone bridge extended like a hand across a murmuring river. Another road ran parallel to ours, and there on the other side of the Carmarthen River stood the town. To our right the countryside stretched before us in all its glory.

It was such a freeing feeling—walking with our bags into a town where we didn't know a soul, or where to go or anything. We wandered into a bed and breakfast that was too expensive. The man there told us about another B&B about five miles from the center of town. So, Christine and I went to the taxi garage to try to get to the Traveler's Inn Guest House. The taxi station had exactly four cars: two that worked, one that was out of commission, and one hearse. The owner of the cab company called Traveler's Inn for us and discovered that they charged £32 per night! So we staggered back to the main street and inquired in the Ansel B&B. I was just about to

give an Academy Award-winning performance as a
desperate refugee when the woman finally pointed out to
me that she charged only £10 pounds per night! We
became guests at the Ansel Inn.

The decor: a tacky fake oil painting of two white
horses near a stream. And the heating unit in my room
looked like either a progressive toaster or a radiation-
ridden torture device!

The two of us threw our stuff down and set out.
Finding an outdoor market and a grocery store, we
bought a large loaf of dark wheat bread, peanut butter
(what else?), jelly, cheddar cheese, fruit juice, and nap-
kins. A steep hill led us from the center of town to a
charming little park. And a rugby match! We sat on a
bench and ate PB&J sandwiches while Christine explained rugby to me and what a violent game it is. As if to
prove her right, a medic ran in from the sidelines once
every, oh, 45 seconds or so. It was cold, but sitting on that
bench, overlooking hills and valleys while the sun slowly
set gave me such a feeling of contentment. Done with our
food and getting cold, we decided to keep walking.

Many quaint Welsh houses, gardens with flowers in
full bloom, stone walls. Houses with cobalt blue trim and
sunflowers in the garden. A starkly white church, with a
tall sharp roof, incredibly thin, icicle-like painted arches,
and the most amazing icicle-like tower at the top, which
allowed the light to bounce out with the force with which
it entered: a bright shaft, white hitting white, a beam
shooting out into the whiteness of the air.

We came back to the inn, got in our jammies, turned
on the heater, and sat in Chris' room writing letters,
talking and reading; at 7:15 P.M. we were in for the night!

10/31…This morning we got up early, showered, and
Sheila, our friendly Welsh hostess, gave us breakfast. We
found out that for £1.40 we could take a train to Kidwelly,
a village with a castle from the year 1130. The train wasn't

scheduled to leave till 12:30, so we set out on another walk—to a neighboring village that climbs a huge hill from which you can see for miles. We saw cats, an adorable huggable mutt, a stream, sheep on a hillside, fresh damp earth, leaves to crunch on as we stepped. At 11:30 Chris and I were back at the B&B collecting our things and being given a lovely little pamphlet by Sheila and her husband, Cyril.

The train ride took all of 15 minutes! As we walked to the center of the village, a woman stopped her car next to me, asking where we were going, and offered us a ride! Her name was Norma. We drove to the center of town, and she stopped at a charming ice cream shoppe to ask about a B&B for us. Across the street was a B&B, run by two old women who tut-tutted around, preparing one of the beds for us. So Norma suggested we have a coffee at her home while the room was being prepared.

Thus began an amazing three-hour psychological orgy—talking about materialism, prejudice, Norma's life with her late husband and being accepted by his family; her children and her relationship with her daughter; priorities, death, grieving, learning.

"It's important to just go through life with your eyes open," Norma said. "People don't understand that there's a difference between 'Standard of Living' and 'Standard of Life.' As long as I can look out my window and see trees, I'll be happy."

We were thrilled, all three of us. Oh, what can happen when you open yourself up. You have to just leave yourself open to experiences—don't count anything out. We didn't and look at what happened to us.

"Today was so unique," Christine just said to me. And so it was. We saw the sun set from the beautiful churchyard cemetery across the street—the sun going down with the bare trees silhouetted against it, and Kidwelly Castle fitting neatly into the landscape. Smoke curling out of a

new home's chimney—a new home right next to this
Norman castle from the twelfth century. The church bells
toll as I write this. Three horses galloping, and staring at
us from the field. The temperature, with the silent setting
sun, dropped with the darkness. And hunger overtook us
when we discovered the orientally decorated Queen Bee
Restaurant. A wonderful meal served by yet more friendly
Welsh people.

The day can be summed up by this poem by Lu Yu,
from *The Tao of Pooh*:

> *The clouds above us join and separate,*
> *The breeze in the courtyard leaves and returns.*
> *Life is like that so why not relax?*
> *Who can stop us from celebrating?*

The third box from Lockerbie arrives on my birthday, July 3,
1989. A birthday present from the Scottish police. A birthday
present from Miriam. I lift the cover off. There lies her address
book—a history of her friendships over the past five years and
now crammed full of all the new friends she's made abroad. (I
find it useful to this day—she's helping me even now.) The box
also contains a shiny gray book—identical to Heather's, the
second of Miriam's London journals. An excerpt:

10/1/88...I am sitting, as I always sit, on a grassy slope
under a tree—surrounded by infinite shades of green and
yellow. My shoes are off, and I sit Indian style. People
look at me as if I'm odd. It's the most touching and
wonderful park scene I've ever seen. Two middle-aged,
upper-middle-class fathers pushing their infants in
strollers and talking. Old women alone on benches,
dressed in their Sunday best. An elderly couple—the
woman wearing a heavy coat though it's warm. Little dogs
that yap, a playful golden retriever—every dog retrieving
a ball. A squirrel scratching himself in the sunlight. Little

boy with father—skipping with his blue balloon. Two little blond girls with ponytails rollerskating—they're both so graceful. Frisbee players, soccer players. An entire hill with people like me reading, meditating and writing...some on their stomachs, some on their backs, one with a Walkman and a notebook, one with suntan oil. Three soon-to-be delinquents on skateboards making too much noise, obstructing the natural balance. Three Indian boys—one on one bike, two on another—flying. A beautiful stylish man in a long gray coat that flows in the breeze as he walks swiftly away from me. A severe-looking woman in purple pants and a gray blazer buttoned to the neck with her tiny matching gray French poodle.

10/6/88...We're on the coach, on our way out of London, headed for the boat to Amsterdam. There's something about packing up and leaving anywhere that makes me introspective and a little sad. Despite the noncommittal drizzling, it's a beautiful evening. The sky is an icy pastel, and tufts of clouds are vibrant in the sunset. Leaves are finally beginning to fall. Rush hour is about to erupt in full swing.

The Tao of Pooh is having a real effect on me—the whole idea that there's an overall plan for things, and that the more we try to control and interrupt life's natural rhythm the farther we are from the truth—what a concept. It's actually very important for me: the idea that overintellectualizing leaves you with more unanswered (and often irrelevant) questions.

The idea that trying too hard is antiproductive—it goes against my grain, that line of thinking. I know that in certain instances, trying too hard does damage—an overly zealous mother can destroy her children by trying too hard to be the perfect mother. But why is it such a crime to try too hard, to better myself, my relationships with people, my mind, my craft?

If I try to better myself, and am passionate in that, I'm called a "perfectionist"—a supposedly unhealthy category. If I try too hard to better my mind, if I read and spell well as a result, then I'm an intellectual snob, trying to assert my self-congratulatory, superior attitude. (Is it being in theater that makes some of my classmates so anti-intellectual?) And, if I try too hard at my art, I get in my own way. I cease to be natural, released, free, spontaneous.

All children are ever taught is to try: "Try your best," they tell us. But it ends up being detrimental. I don't know how to just exist—it doesn't feel like living. I'm tired of feeling guilty and inferior and stupid because I can't stop trying. What would they have me do? "People-pleasing"—it's turning into a dirty word.

But I have confidence in myself and I'm going to continue doing what I know is best for me. I need to keep reminding myself of what Isadora Duncan said in her book *And She Danced*: "Anyone can dance. Just put your hands to your heart and listen to your soul, and you can dance. But most people are deaf."

Do I feel I'm invading Miriam's privacy by reading her journals? No, I feel they bring me closer to her, because she's always talked so openly to me about everything and we've shared so much. Going through her journals I feel a sense of amazement at the amount she has written, the outpouring of emotion and how much I'm learning about her. Reading her journals is like having a conversation with her. The journals are an extension of herself, as vivacious, as intellectual, and as melodramatic as she was. She's alive in these pages, which are filled with little doodles, drawings, jokes, as well as reflections and quotes.

The *Baltimore Sun* and *The Capital* carry front-page stories about my receiving her journals from Lockerbie. The boxes contain all her London writings. Reading through them,

I ask myself: What have I been missing? What might I find here in her own room? I begin rummaging through her desk drawers. From her closet I pull out cartons of her college and high school papers. I come upon a required journal that she kept for her "core" drama class at Syracuse. I find long-forgotten grade school papers, poems, wonderful art work, little diaries. Discovering her through these pages gives me enormous comfort—and distress too: a diary entry when she was upset—she wasn't getting the attention she wanted from a boy she liked; it makes me hurt too.

In her closet I discover Miriam the activist—a placard she carried when she attended a pro-choice rally in Washington. On the back she'd written: "March 1987, my first protest march!"

In the musical *Mame*, there's a song "Open a New Window, Open a New Door." The boxes from Lockerbie introduce me to my daughter all over again. And sitting on the lime green rug in her room, I decide to write a book that will capture her spirit. Thus begins what will turn out to be my quest to immortalize my daughter.

In London she had bought no fewer than forty books. Many were textbooks and guidebooks, of course, but other titles reflect a gigantic thirst for learning and a huge range of interests, especially art, literature, drama, and philosophy. *Love* by Leo Buscaglia, *A Critical Dictionary of Psychoanalysis*, *Guide to Yoga*, Shakespeare's sonnets. Miriam herself was something of a mystic and philosopher—a side of her I had not yet really begun to know.

I find no fewer than three copies of *The Tao of Pooh*, a book I'd never even heard of until she mentioned it many times in her journals. Given that our favorite book to read together was *Winnie-the-Pooh*, I quickly open it and learn what she meant about "life's natural rhythm"—how man so often disrupts the heavenly harmony of the universe. But suddenly I can read no more. I think of the letter from her friend that Charles Kuralt read on *Sunday Morning*: "There is now a serious imbalance in the universe: Miriam Wolfe was aboard Pan Am Flight 103." It is not God's will that Miriam lies in a cemetery.

From this day on, Miriam's books become living, breathing things for me. The shelves are alive! Each time I look through the bookcases I discover something I don't remember ever seeing before. *Auto Repair for Dummies, The Two Sources of Morality and Religion, Postcards From the Edge*—when did those get there? I didn't see them yesterday, and I go into her room almost every day—to wrap a gift, to get one of my dresses out of her closet. It's almost otherworldly.

She speaks to me through her books. There is *Zen and the Art of Motorcycle Maintenance*. Twenty years ago, I thought of it as a hippy book and my conservative side dismissed it. But now I try again, searching for what Miriam might have seen in it. What I discover is a profoundly moving story of a father and young son who had a difficult relationship—and how their cross-country journey brings them in touch with nature, themselves, and each other.

And *Act I* by Moss Hart—such an absorbing portrait of life in the theater. Oh, how I wish I'd read it when Miriam was alive. He says: "Temperament is little else than a mask for panic, and when people are panic-stricken, they of course behave badly. Why should they not?" I recall all the hours, days even, before opening nights when Miriam stomped around the house—so irritable, so difficult, and how annoyed she made me. She had stage fright, pure and simple.

The boxes from Lockerbie overflow with art books. During one of her phone calls from London, she told me, "I just might get a Ph.D. in art history someday." Images of art often fill my mind when I think of Miriam. She was a swirl of Renoir pastels. Or a mosaic, a thousand rainbow facets melted into a vibrant reality. In high school, on the days I thought she'd never get to class on time, she was a Kandinsky, an abstract burst of frenzied colors rushing to catch the yellow school bus.

But now, in the blackest pigment of night, paintings crack

and dissipate. Mary Cassatt's tender mother sits on the beach without her child. Renoir's mother in a blue dress now has no little hand to hold. In a Gainsborough family portrait, only a gaping emptiness remains where the daughter once stood.

Peeking out from among the art books is a white plastic bag on which Miriam had written, all in caps, in red pen: "STUFF TO LOOK AT WHEN YOU THINK NO ONE LOVES YOU!" Inside are forty-three letters, postcards, and birthday cards from friends and family, including all ten of my letters.

At the bottom of the last box from Lockerbie, I find one of the last papers she wrote in London. I scan it. Oh, oh, this is the bottom of the barrel—for me personally, that is. I'm thinking I have a lot to learn about my daughter's attitude toward me. Maybe I don't need to know everything, I tell myself. Maybe I won't read it. But of course I do. Over and over. The paper discusses a play about a famed child psychoanalyst. But it's also about the two of us.

Mrs. Klein

The production of *Mrs. Klein* by Nicholas Wright at the National Theatre had a tremendous impact on me and forced me to seriously reanalyze many aspects of my life. Though psychoanalysis may be a remote subject for some, it is very much a part of my makeup. My grandfather, who is probably my biggest source of inspiration, is 84 years old and is a practicing psychoanalyst. His concern, like Melanie Klein's, is Freudian psychoanalysis. Not surprisingly, my grandfather's involvement in this aspect of medicine has had a profound effect on both my mother and me.

In the NT production, Melanie Klein destroys her relationship with her daughter, Melitta, because of an inability to stop acting as a psychoanalyst. Mrs. Klein has a cold, analytical approach to virtually every facet of her life, including her relationship with her children. This may seem imperceptible at first. But, once one is educat-

ed in psychiatric terminology, it's very easy to let Melanie
Klein's problem get the best of you.

I identified very strongly with the character of Melitta. She is still struggling to find her identity—an identity
separate from the one she knows with her mother. The
fact that Melitta and Mrs. Klein are colleagues as well as
mother and daughter complicates matters severely.
Melitta was stripped of her self-worth as a child. She is
also obsessed with winning her mother's approval, even
though she knows intellectually that this is a futile effort.
All of these factors contribute to making Melitta an
extraordinarily complex and neurotic woman.

Naturally, my grandfather taught his children (my
mother and her brother) the importance of self-aware-
ness. This, in turn, has had a significant effect on my
mother's relationship with me. My mother, in an attempt
to instill in me a strong sense of self, raised me as an
equal. She did not take the authoritarian role. This
resulted in the development of a complex relationship
which has included my struggle for an identity separate
from my mother. For nine years, my mother and I lived
alone together—and for obvious reasons are exceptionally
close.

My grandfather's professional status has made me
particularly aware of my motives for doing certain things.
Recently, I have come to understand the psychological
reasons for my constant search for mentors in older, more
successful women. This search is a direct result of not
having grown up worshipping my mother. I had respect
for her, certainly. But because we were more like sisters
than mother and daughter, I never went through the
"normal" psychological process of thinking that my
parents, particularly my mother, were perfect. So, I tried
to transfer my stifled feelings onto other adult women
whom I could emulate. *Mrs. Klein* actually had a great
deal to do with this realization.

Mrs. Klein also illustrates the frustration and unhappiness that sometimes accompany knowing a lot about one's own psychology. It becomes very difficult to act as a human being, without stopping to recognize, analyze, and reanalyze the motivation behind the action.

As I tuck *Mrs. Klein* back in the box, I grudgingly admire Miriam's intellect and at the same time wish I'd been the perfect mother. Wouldn't we all like to be? The exhilaration of climbing into my daughter's head through her writings has its flip side; it reinforces what I've always known: that her sensitivity and insight produced a painful share of agonies and conflicts. But the flip side is something deeper and less selfish for me. I'd gladly take a dozen of her papers examining our relationship. The really tough part for me is, first, the knowledge that there will never be any more of her writings. But far worse is the knowledge that there's no more "us." Miriam was twenty when she died. I was twenty-one when my mother died. All three of us have been deprived of each other—the dialogues; the realness of arguments and exasperations; the struggle to understand one another and yet create our own sphere of independence; the comfort we would have given each other for years to come.

What I'm to discover is that comfort comes from unexpected places and that these voices can become a source of peace.

CHAPTER NINE

Music to My Ears

STANDING on our front porch is an anxious-looking young woman, who hands me a long-stemmed pink rose.

"I just couldn't come before this," she says, her voice shaking. It's been eight months since Miriam died.

"That's all right," I reply, holding the door for her. "I knew you'd come eventually."

We sit in the living room and reminisce. She had arrived at Miriam's school in fourth grade, mature for her age, and an exceptionally gifted musician. With the almost predictable cruelty of kids, many classmates snubbed her for being different.

"I didn't think I'd be able to survive that year," she says. "Miriam made me feel I was worthy of being somebody's friend. When we sat together on top of the jungle gym and talked, I knew I was special." They remained friends over the years.

Since Miriam's death, we've received nearly a thousand letters. I read and appreciate them all—some many times over. Of course, the expected condolences and kindnesses prevail, but the numbers and distances stagger our imaginations. Before long, something more begins to emerge, a theme repeated over and over again—so many writing of a gift Miriam had left with them. She had affected their lives by way of encouragement, by way of understanding, by way of enlightenment. I thought I knew my daughter well, but I'm discovering I hardly knew her at all.

At Bay Country Camp for the Theatre Arts, she forged

friendships with other campers, the teachers, and even Sharon Wyrrick, the camp coordinator. Miriam was only fourteen. It didn't matter to her that the staff members were adults; it was her philosophy that if *she* liked *them* they would be her friends.

Sharon is also a well-known dancer and choreographer. In June 1989, the *Washington Post* carried a rave review of her newest work:

"Wyrrick is...one of the most gifted choreographers hereabouts...'Storyboard for an Anxious Journey' [projects] a haunting and disquieting sense of mystery. We've seen it in her earlier works, but never more poignantly than in this work, which among other things is a dirge for a young friend who perished aboard the ill-fated Pan Am Flight 103."

Sharon dedicated the work to Miriam and told me: "Nothing I've ever done has been so well received. Miriam gave me a gift."

From camper to counselor at London Town colonial history camp, she continued to give. Here's one of many such letters:

"When Elizabeth, our daughter, was a camper at London Town, every day was a wonderful experience because Miriam was her counselor....We went to see her in *The Music Man* at Baldwin Hall. After the play, she took Elizabeth backstage, a real thrill to an eight-year-old. Since that memorable summer, Elizabeth has spoken often of Miriam, remembering how kind and cheerful she was—a wonderful example for a little girl to look up to."

Senior year, after Miriam finished a course in constitutional law, the teacher wrote her: "Your commitment to learning has been a huge factor in my maintaining some optimism about education. Please never abandon your convictions, integrity, and capacity for greatness which make you so unique."

"No one who worked with Miriam will ever forget her," the director of Children's Theatre of Annapolis wrote. "She was the ideal model of what CTA is all about. As an actress, she was a perfect professional. She worked hard to give the very best performance she could. And she was a constant source of support and encouragement to others in the show. Her enthusiasm quickly spread to everyone around her. At auditions, while waiting for her turn, she bounced constantly from one group of youngsters to another, first wishing one boy luck, then telling another performer what a good job they had done, next giving another child some ideas on how to do better. At the same time, she would constantly watch for ways to improve her own audition...."

Notes from Syracuse:
    "Miriam was a beacon of love and energy in the class she took with me, a difficult music appreciation class. She was that rare kind of individual who takes such great delight in their growth, both personal and intellectual, that they act as a catalyst for the growth of others."   —A. Waggoner, SU Professor of Music.
    "I was a shy, scared theater major in 1986 and a certain misfit down at the stages. Miriam made me feel comfortable, liked even. I remember her smile, her easy laugh, sitting next to her in Choral Union and our talks at Baskin Robbins. She had a quiet friendly joy that touched my frightened heart and made me grin."   —Lynn.
    "Miriam grabbed everyone around her and forced us all to live and to laugh. I'll never forget our lollipops and gossip sessions and the way she went out and bought Mr. Potato Head."
    —Tracey.

And a letter from London reflecting the thoughts of all her teachers who wrote us:

I am the teaching assistant for the Art History course in London.... Miriam had a complex mind for her age and it was marvelous to watch her playing with new ideas as she tried to make sense of the world....

Early in December we ventured on a field trip to
Birmingham Museum to see Pre-Raphaelite paintings.
During the three-hour coach journey, Miriam chatted,
disclosing her desire to become so many things: an
actress, a playwright, a director, and feared that she
would not be able to realize all these ambitions.... She
was socially aware and wished to write plays that would
stir hearts and minds to act for good in this world. Igno-
rance appalled Miriam. She was also very proud to be
Jewish and was against all forms of discrimination.

She was extremely proud of her family and grateful for
the environment in which she had been nurtured as a child,
one in which discussion was important. She was the kind of
student that makes teaching a rewarding occupation.
    —V. Button.

As Miriam has said, Grandpa Saul influenced her more than
anyone else. My father was her friend, mentor, and role model, exuding humor and warmth, which made his constructive
criticism palatable (and there was plenty of it). They had a private joke. When he called he'd ask:

"So, Miriam, how are you doing in reform school?"

She'd reply: "Well, Grandpa, in my time off for good behavior, I'm doing a little acting, singing...."

One of his patients gave him the following quotation,
framed; it sums up the way he lived his life and the way he
taught Miriam to live hers:

I expect to pass through life but once. If therefore there
be any kindness I can show, or any good thing I can do to
any fellow being, let me do it now, and not defer or
neglect it, as I shall not pass this way again.
    —William Penn

She had been at Syracuse only a month when she called me,
her voice filled with distress. "Mom, I have this friend who

never eats. She keeps saying she just has to lose ten more pounds and then she'll feel better about herself. But I can tell she's starving herself. And in class today she fainted. She's anorexic, Mom. So after class I talked to the teacher."

The responsive teacher immediately arranged for the friend to get counseling. Soon after, the self-destructive behavior stopped—and she did truly begin to feel better about herself.

This was not the first time Miriam tried to help a friend in trouble. I was collecting the carpool of fourteen-year-olds after a play audition. When I arrived I found only one kid standing on the sidewalk waiting. He told me one of the girls had started crying hysterically because she didn't get a part. She'd broken away from the group and run three blocks down the dark street. Miriam and her friends had run after her. As I pulled up to the curb, I saw them huddled around the sobbing girl, trying to comfort her. Her crying continued all the way to her house. I barely had time to put on the brakes when Miriam, herself in tears, jumped out and ran straight into the kitchen.

"Something is very wrong," she blurted out to the girl's mother. "You have to do something. She's gone overboard." Several years later, the child attempted suicide—unsuccessfully, thank God. She's now happily married.

And another incident in high school: The younger sister of a friend whispered to her: "Everything's so lousy, I feel like jumping out a window." Miriam promptly alerted a guidance counselor, who set the wheels in motion for the girl to get into therapy.

Over and over I've heard a familiar chorus… "Because of your daughter…" At a Colonial Players production in Annapolis: "It's because of Miriam that I'm here," an adult cast member told Larry and me. "She encouraged me to get back into acting. I had missed it so."

"Don't ever give up your music, Donna," she told my friend. "You have such a beautiful voice." Choral singing is an essential part of Donna's life today.

•

Probably her most important activity in London was her formation of a new "alternative" theater group to bring back to the Syracuse Drama Department. With her close friend Theo Cohen and several other students, they sought to expand the department's traditional horizons. After Pan Am 103, the students who survived carried on and performed a play to introduce their new vision. One member of the group, Annie Lareau, explained in the program:

"The Add Libb Theatre Company is the product of a great desire to explore new theatrical venues and styles.... Theo and Miriam were the two brain children of the group. It was their hunger for political issues to be discussed through theater and brought to not only the department, but also the general public. They felt strongly that if theater was to survive it needed to reach fresh audiences. 'Theater is not just for theater people,' Miriam Wolfe said. The five of us set out to bring what we dreamed of being physical theater—mime, improvisation, playwrighting seminars and guest speakers—to the department, to the campus at large, and ideally to the more impoverished parts of Syracuse...."

When Miriam's London roommate Jessica Frankel comes to visit us, she talks about their life in London: "Miriam saw an old man in the street. He appeared confused and lost. She asked him where he wanted to go and put him in a taxi. She loved helping people. She also helped me decide what to do after graduation."

"Try the Milwaukee Repertory Company, they have internships," Miriam suggested. "Use me as a reference." Miriam had been to Milwaukee in the spring of '88 to visit my father and they had taken a tour through the theater. She had quickly developed a rapport with the director and sent her a postcard from London. Jessica spent several successful runs with the company.

Miriam wrote the following letter to her fifteen-year-old step-brother, Chris Spencer, when she was a freshman at Syracuse. Three years older than Chris, she wanted to spare him some of the agonies of the college application process. P.S. Chris was accepted into and graduated from his first-choice college as an architecture major.

How to Apply to College: A Sister's Advice

The closer we get to Fall, the closer the college application process gets. And I remember what a frenzy I was in when I was going through the business of applying to schools. So, I decided to write you a letter that passes on all the stuff I learned from my experience. I hope it helps.

O.K., here we go.

A Few General Points to Remember:

1. *Nothing is written in stone,* which means that if you don't get into your first choice school, you can always apply as a transfer student after one year somewhere else. So, don't let any of this stuff overwhelm you. No matter what anyone tells you, this is not a life and death decision.

2. When looking at colleges, remember to consider more than just what you plan to major in. Make sure that if you choose a school for architecture it also will be a place where you can (a) play your trumpet, (b) play sports that are important to you, etc. Make sure you'll be able to do recreation type things that you enjoy.

3. Consider the size of the school (which, of course, affects classroom size), the location, and the people. The people are probably the most important thing, because the people you go to college with really do have a big influence on your values and ideas for the rest of your life.

That's why it's important, if at all possible, to *visit the schools you are considering!!* That way, you can decide what the school's really like. Please remember that the college brochures only tell their side of the story—they want to sell you on their school and they try to make you see it with rose-colored glasses. So, when you visit, ask if you can sit in on a class or two.

At my high school, seniors were allowed to visit colleges, and it was considered an excused absence. You may want to find out if that's true at your school.

4. One of the things that makes the application process such a pain is that *You have to "toot your own horn!"*

The thing that gets you into colleges is the thing they notice about you that is *different* from the other thousands of kids who apply. So, you have to emphasize the fact that you successfully completed two college-level architecture courses in your junior and senior years. Then, it won't matter as much if you don't have 1500 SAT scores. Seriously, Chris, that's the name of the game.

Emphasize your accomplishments, especially all the Band stuff. They like to see that kids can stick to something and do it well. Your accomplishments in that area will impress them.

O.K., now let's talk about what to do in the early stages of applying to schools, which means September to December of your senior year.

1. Get recommendations from teachers and counselors done early. Why? Because they will get swamped with requests. Chances are, the teachers you choose to write recommendations for you are some of the best teachers in the school, which is why lots of kids'll be after 'em. The sooner they write your recommendation, the more specific they'll be about you, and the more flattering their reports of you will be. After teachers write enough recommendations, they tend to get generic with their answers, which is the last thing you need. You want yours to sound different from the other 4,000 any college may receive.

2. Most schools give their applicants the option of having an interview. Interviews work in one of two ways: you either interview at the school itself, or you do an "alumni" interview (an interview in your home town with a graduate of the school). Generally, interviews at the school itself carry more weight than alum ones, because they're conducted by the actual staff...the Dean of Admissions, etc. (But alum interviews are better than nothing.)

Why are interviews important??

Because they show that you (a) are a person with direction, (b) are articulate, (c) are a genuine, honest, sweet guy. They can't hurt—it's important to stress your individuality, so, unless the idea of an interview situation really bothers you, I'd give it a whirl.

3. Lastly, it's really important to make every college think that it is your first choice. What I mean by this is, take care with every application. Don't let on, from the way your application looks, that you've taken any less care than if it were another school.

Don't forget to apply to some safety schools (schools you know you'll get into). You want to make sure you give yourself as many options as possible.

Most of all, Chris, please try to remember that everything happens for a reason. Everything will work out for the best. Just do the best you can, and be gentle with yourself. Please don't hesitate to call me if you have a question, or just need to talk. I remember this whole scene very clearly.

No matter what, do what's best for you. Your parents will love you no matter what you do. And, of course, so will I. I'm sooo proud of you. I also miss you a great deal.

So, dear brother, I'll sign off.... With All My Love, Miriam

The *Washington Post* published her letter in Style Plus on December 4, 1992. It touched off a wave of letters from kids, parents, and teachers telling us how valuable her advice had been. High school guidance counselors posted it on their bulletin boards. And on April 27, 1997, the letter was published again in a special college section in the *New York Daily News*.

It has been said that a grain of poetry suffices to season a century. More than ten years after she wrote it, Miriam's letter is nurturing a whole new generation.

CHAPTER TEN

Thanks for Everything, Miriam, I Miss You

by Jake Stigers

I met Miriam Wolfe in June of 1988. We had summer jobs performing in shows at Darien Lake, an amusement park near Buffalo, New York. My show was a Broadway revue and hers was a pop show, comprising popular music from the last four decades.

We discovered each other right away in rehearsals and became close friends almost instantly. Alone in a strange new city, Miriam and I were relieved to find at least one genuine friend with whom to spend the summer. We were also excited to find, in each other, a friend who shared the same cultural and intellectual interests.

We spent most of our free time together those three months comparing opinions about great literature, renting cultural movies, reciting Carol Burnett scenes, visiting the Albright-Knox Art Gallery in Buffalo, finding profound quotes to send backstage to each other (Macbeth's 'Life's but a walking shadow' remains my favorite), making fun of the abhorrent spelling in the park newsletter (Did'nt...Hawiin...Manhatten) and counting the days until our jobs would finally be finished.

Miriam and I didn't agree on everything, though. She was an ardent feminist, and much to her chagrin, I had only a passing interest in the feminist cause. We often had heated disagreements over the relative importance of many works of literature or current events. The two of us also didn't see eye-to-eye regarding Dustin Hoffman's ability as an actor. She thought he was talented. Before I met Miriam, I considered any disagreement between friends a manifestation of personal hatred. I could not be friends with someone with whom I did not share almost the same opinions and values. Needless to say, I had few true, close friends. Miriam showed me that friends can disagree, and that often an argument can lead to an education or a strengthening of a relationship.

Miriam exposed me to a lot that summer. She introduced me to the joys of discussing literature and musical theater over baked brie and white zinfandel. She whiled away most of her free time between her shows plowing through Ayn Rand's *The Fountainhead*, a weighty tome that only began to whet her insatiable appetite for mental stimulation. Miriam couldn't believe I had never, as an English major, heard of Rainer Maria Rilke's *Letters to a Young Poet*, and she gave me her very own copy to make sure I would have this book in my personal library.

When summer finally ended, I assumed we would remain faithful pen pals at best and maybe not see each other for at least a few years, as is normally the case with the friends one makes while working in theme park shows around the country.

After the fall semester was well under way, I was delighted to get an overseas call one afternoon from her. She had missed me and just wanted to hear my voice. We chatted for a few expensive, precious minutes and joked that it would be great if I could somehow visit her in London. I must have later mentioned that conversation to my mom, because a few days later, completely out of character, she told me that I "only live once" and I should go to visit Miriam. I quickly ordered a passport and called Miriam to tell her she was to have company.

I arrived in London's Gatwick airport at 9 A.M. after a freezing and sleepless flight over the Atlantic. From somewhere to my right, I heard a cheerful salutation, "Jake, my dear! How are you?" I turned my head and instantly saw Miriam. She was practically doing handsprings to get my attention.

Let me digress a second here. You know those toy dolls with the strings you pull that make their arms and legs flail spastically? Imagine one of those dolls with the trademark buoyant Muppet walk and a head of big, bouncy curls that accent each exuberant body movement. Now add a sophisticated Barbra Streisand nose, a perpetually cheery grin with a slight head tilt and a practical-yet-classic (size six) wardrobe from, say, the Gap. That's Miriam.

We ran to see each other and hugged for what seemed to be twenty minutes. After we realized we were in the way of the other passengers, we walked to the in-airport train station arm-in-arm, talking all the time. We caught up on gossip about the people we had worked with the summer before as we rode the train to the London tube station and once we had debarked, we broke into fits of giggles as we realized we had probably shocked the people around us with the scandalous nature of our conversation.

At the tube station we waited in line, still gossiping and giggling, so I could buy a week-long tube pass. The man in front of us got into a fight with the ticket seller over some discrepancy in change and shouted angrily in a genuine cockney accent, "Piss off!" Miriam turned to me with the biggest grin on her face and said in her best cockney, "Welcome to London!" Our gales of laughter no doubt betrayed the fact that we were genuine tourists.

Thus began my fast-paced, incredible week in London. The first place Miriam took me that morning, after we had dumped my stuff at her Kensington Park flat, was the Museum of the Moving Image, a fascinating exhibit of the history of filmmaking. Halfway through the museum I suddenly felt a rush of uncontrollable exhaustion. Yup. Jet lag. Miriam somehow steered me back to her flat for a long nap. We tried again the next day, after having spent a leisurely afternoon in the flat and having eaten a tasteless dinner at a trendy European vegetarian restaurant.

Before the week was over, we had spent significant amounts of time in four art museums, including the Wallace Collection, an obscure little private gallery where Jean-Honore Fragonard's *The Swing* hangs. Miriam and I shared a mutual passion for Rococo art, and *The Swing* was one of our favorite works. She just happened to know it was housed at this quaint little museum. Once we were finally standing together before our painting, displayed in an exquisite Victorian setting, our perpetual giggling stopped and all we could do was stand in awe and allow the passionate swirls of color emanating from the canvas to bathe us in their intricate, breathtaking beauty. We had to come back to gaze at it four more times before we decided to leave the museum. Before we left, though, we each bought expensive prints of the work in the museum gift shop and I was elected to carry them carefully for the next eight hours of sightseeing in downtown London. I even had to bring them with us to high tea at Harrod's. Though we desperately tried not to look like tourists, the two cumbersome tubes I carried and our gales of laughter at the blandness of the local highbrow cuisine (scones and clotted butter) no doubt gave us away.

Miriam and I also took in three shows that week (including a breathtaking *Les Miserables* and Stephen Sondheim's *Follies*) and attended Mass in an awe-inspiring cathedral (though her family is Jewish and mine is Protestant). We even had lunch in an authentic pub and made Thanksgiving dinner with some of her friends from school in their flat—in the same building where (then) internationally famous pop singer George Michael lived.

Miriam and I both love language and grammar, and we were perpetually amused by the odd constructions and foreign trends in European advertising as we read the posters on the tube. Our favorite joke concerned the tear-jerking narratives of convicted "fare fiddlers," people who try to ride the tube without paying.

We spent one of my last nights in London in an enormous

old bookstore. As we explored the tall dark aisles of shelving, I came across a book that had changed my ways of thinking: John Berger's *Ways of Seeing*, a fascinating collection of essays on perception and subliminalism in society. I brought the book to Miriam's attention, expecting her already to have read and dissected it in countless literature and art classes. To my complete shock, she hadn't. I made her buy it and promise to read it before she reached the States in December. A few aisles later, we encountered Sally Swain's *Great Housewives of Art*, a feminist repainting of Western art from the last three centuries. Since the book doubled us over in laughter, we each bought a copy.

My too-short visit in London over, Miriam and I exchanged tearful farewells and promised to write as soon as we could. The last time I saw her she was standing on a little boulevard in the street. Her roommates had given us a terrible time about the fact that we both owned black penny loafers, so we made sure we always wore them together. She was grinning and jumping around and waving to me as my taxi whisked me to the tube station that would take me to Heathrow Airport. I made it home safely and got caught up in schoolwork as if nothing exciting had happened in my life. Miriam and I wrote each other quite a lot and called with even more frequency than before, our recent reunion reminding us of the fact that we missed each other so much.

On the morning of December 21, my semester finals all safely behind me, my dad picked me up at school to take me home for Christmas vacation. As we pulled into the driveway, my mother appeared beside the car, crying and shaking uncontrollably. Through her sobs she told us: Miriam's plane went down.

We walked slowly into the house. I told myself that I didn't know anything for sure, so I refused to get emotional. My Dad turned on CNN and my family stared in numb helplessness at television footage of the plane wreckage strewn about Lockerbie, Scotland.

Life went on the next eight months. Accepting Miriam's death wasn't impossibly difficult for me because, all alone in Iowa, I certainly wasn't used to seeing her all the time so I didn't suddenly have a void in my life in her absence. I miss her most whenever some reminder of one of our countless inside jokes comes to my attention and I realize I really can't call her any more to share in my laughter.

Sunday, September 10, 1989, I finally made it to Severna Park to visit Miriam's family. Her mother and I went through some of Miriam's things that had been recovered from the 845-square-mile crash site. I was shocked to find *Ways of Seeing* and *Great Housewives of Art* among those recovered items. They were waterlogged and covered with Scottish dirt, but they had survived the crash.

We went to the cemetery so I could have an official goodbye. The rectangle of half-dead sod that covered her new grave seemed to me to be a morbid joke. How could Miriam's body, perpetually in a state of exuberant motion, be dead and buried? There seemed no possible way that that brown turf and that gravestone could hold her still.

It is an uncomfortable feeling to lose a friend in an international tragedy. I can be driven to an overwhelming state of grief whenever a story about the crash appears on the news. Miriam had had a dramatic and commanding presence while she lived. Hers was a full, rich life and she certainly made a mark on many other lives. Perhaps the only way for a visible, essential person such as Miriam to go would be in a way that the whole world would know about it. Her final curtain call had international coverage and will be recalled for years to come when other planes are brought down by terrorists' bombs.

Thanks for everything, Miriam. I miss you.

Jake composed this essay for a college writing class. A 1990 graduate of the University of Iowa, he is now an award-winning advertising copywriter and freelance writer, who has published in Time, U.S. News & World Report, *the* Cedar Rapids Gazette, *and elsewhere. His essay "Surviving the Bombing of Pan Am Flight 103: The Loss of Innocence and a Dear Friend in an International Tragedy" was published in the January–March 1998 issue of the* Journal of Personal & Interpersonal Loss.

CHAPTER ELEVEN

From Mourning to Lobbying

JANUARY 18, 1989, in Syracuse, New York, the bitter cold expresses our collective mood. We're gathered together in a Sheraton suite, the families of the thirty-five Syracuse University students killed aboard Pan Am 103. Most of us are meeting each other for the first time. We're gathered in sorrow and for solace for a milestone event the next day—the university service to memorialize our children. We talk with other families and hear their stories. The camaraderie comforts us. For the first time, we feel we are not alone.

More than 10,000 students and faculty attend the solemn SU service in the Carrier Dome, which concludes with an impassioned good-bye to each of our children. At Hendricks Chapel thirty-five memorial books, each one bearing the student's name in gold, are set out on tables lit by candles. Friends, faculty, and parents stand in long lines to write their thoughts and farewells.

This same night, seven families attend a special Drama Department memorial service. For three hours, drama students and faculty move us to emotions we never thought possible with original songs, dances, poems, and memories. These talented friends bring us through an entire range of feelings, sharing their friendship and love. Through our tears we're startled to find ourselves even laughing about our kids' quirks and escapades. One of Miriam's friends from home reminisces about "the Maryland Miriam":

"Mir loved the piano bar we used to frequent at a pub

called Marmaduke's. It was always our first date when we got back from SU. She loved to get up and sing "Cockeyed Optimist" from *South Pacific* or "Don't Cry for Me, Argentina" from *Evita*. She always sang beautifully, but it didn't matter—she would always come back to the table, sit down, and brood about every mistake she had made in the song."

I break out into helpless laughter. She was such a perfectionist. He's captured her exactly.

Afterward, at a reception for the Drama Department families, the university dean hands me a card—Miriam made the Dean's List. Actually, she had made straight A's. Syracuse will establish thirty-five scholarships in perpetuity, one for each student lost, as well as a marble memorial wall at the gates of the university.

When Pan Am 103 exploded over foreign soil, there were 183 Americans on board. We had every reason to believe our State Department had procedures in place for handling an international catastrophe like ours with speed and sensitivity. Right? Wrong. The State Department had no system for notifying next of kin—nor for even obtaining a copy of the airline manifest, for that matter. On December 21, that blackest of days, Pan Am didn't call us and neither did the State Department. Weeks later, when identified bodies were finally shipped home, the families awaiting their loved ones' remains at JFK found themselves in a humiliating and degrading situation. The bodies had been transported like cattle to a cargo area of the airport. We personally were spared that humiliation.

Thus, the families have congregated in the Syracuse hotel suite not just for comfort, but with a second aim in mind. A political aim. Outraged at our government's inaction and insensitivity, intensely angered by Pan Am's behavior, we have united to form the Victims of Pan Am Flight 103 (VPAF103). We are drawn together not only by grief, but also by frustrated efforts directed at the airline, the FAA, and the State Department. VPAF103 will become a powerful, effective lobbying group.

Labeling ourselves "victims" is not an arbitrary decision. The Justice Department defines a victim as a person who has suffered direct or threatened physical, emotional, or monetary harm as a result of the commission of a crime. In the case of a victim who is deceased, the following are also considered victims: a spouse, a parent, a legal guardian, a child, a sibling, another family member or any person designated by the court.

Our new group spells out its goals. We ask the State Department to return the remains not yet received as well as our loved ones' personal effects in an expeditious, humane manner. This is part of our grand design: to secure victims' rights and to correct flaws in the system that led to insensitive, abusive treatment of the surviving families. We also plan to serve as a victims' support group and source of information to the families.

We call for a government investigation to determine all those responsible for such a horrendous crime and how it was carried out. We also demand a separate concurrent government investigation into how an informed government and a prestigious, worldwide American-based carrier permitted this tragedy to occur. Could it have been avoided? Were there mistakes, wrongful procedures, and negligence that created the climate for such a crime? Results of the investigation will lay the groundwork for future legislation for improved airport security. We want to ensure that a Pan Am 103 will never happen again.

At this first meeting on January 18, Larry and I distribute copies of our op-ed piece published in the *Baltimore Sun* on January 6:

Six Proposals on Airplane Terrorism
With the loss of our beloved Miriam…we present six suggestions to help prevent future acts of terrorism.

(1) This plea we direct at the media: Articles that give public recognition to individual terrorists and the groups or ideals they serve further the terrorist's purpose—as a child smashes a toy in order to obtain parental attention.

We suggest that the phrase "an identified terrorist or fanatical group has claimed credit" be substituted for any actual known names....

(2) ...We propose an international agreement among manufacturers to provide plastic explosives with an odor additive within the sensory range of specially trained dogs and a trace of radioactive ingredient within the sensory range of ordinary detection instruments. These additives would go a long way toward the prevention of transportation bombings.

(3)...The luggage compartments of aircraft could be isolated by a blast-proof shield and vented outward for the expanding gases normally associated with an explosion. The compartment itself could be jettisoned to restore fly-ability and control.

(4) Once luggage is inspected, each piece should be marked with a large paper stick-on band that would encompass the entire article. A numbered passenger along with numbered luggage would make last-minute switching more difficult.

Carry-on luggage should be further limited in size and similarly numbered. In the cabin, closed-circuit TV cameras wired to blast-protected (in-flight) recorders might reveal strange activity preceding an act of on-board terrorism and lead to insight for future adjustments. This scheme apparently works in the banking system.

(5)...From mid-afternoon on that fateful Wednesday until after midnight we were unable to determine whether our Miriam was actually on board.... Friends, relatives, well-wishers and, of course, the media, occupied the phone lines and turned that evening into a nightmare of redialings.... We believe a standing task force—of the U.S. State Department for international flights and the FAA for domestic flights—should step in immediately and establish channels to the next-of-kin without fear of legal repercussions or incurring liability....

(6) Lastly, let there be an agency whose sole purpose is to solicit and examine ideas from just plain people.... It is too late to prevent the death of our dear Miriam, but if one life can be saved by one of our thoughts, the fact that she inspired it will give proof that she lived and will continue to live in our hearts.

Maryland Senator Barbara Mikulski enters our editorial into the *Congressional Record* and sends copies to William Sessions, then Director of the FBI, and to Rep. Dante Fascell, Chairman of the House Committee on Foreign Relations. Rep. Sessions forwards a copy to the head of the FAA. Rep. Fascell writes to thank us.

President Ronald Reagan had one more month in office when Pan Am 103 exploded. Yet he issued not one word of condolence to the families, either public or private. (An ugly rumor surfaced that President Reagan and Prime Minister Margaret Thatcher spoke on the phone and decided to downplay the disaster. The rumor was never confirmed.)

On a wintry February afternoon, VPAF103 gathers at Lafayette Park directly across the road from the White House. We heap flowers on a temporary shrine and state our purpose: to protest our government's lack of action. President Bush is now in office. He too is silent.

It is at Lafayette Park that my friendship begins with Peggy and Ann, Maryland residents whose daughters were among the Syracuse students on the plane. We feel an immediate kinship. VPAF103 begins to feel a new sense of empowerment. We establish a newsletter. The families are firmly connected. Many members take an active political role in getting our voices heard. They begin to haunt the halls of Congress.

Belatedly, in direct response to the families' protests, on April 6, 1989, President Bush sends a condolence letter to each family, vowing to "identify the cowardly murderers" and improve airport security. Responding to the unyielding determination of the families, he issues, on August 4, 1989, an Executive Order forming the seven-member President's Commission on Aviation Security and Terrorism. Ann McLaughlin, former U.S. Secretary of Labor, chairs the Commission, which also includes two senators, two congressmen, a former Secretary of the Navy and a just-retired Air Force general. For six months, the Commission conducts a thorough review of existing security, options for handling terrorist threats, and the treatment of victims.

On May 15, 1990, the families are ushered through the security checkpoint into the imposing Executive Office Building. We've been invited to a State Department briefing of the Commission's findings. President Bush speaks briefly, questions are answered, and each family receives a copy of the report and an American flag. The flags are given in the same spirit as those given to military dead—because a crime has been committed against the United States, not merely against individuals. A hushed, heavy atmosphere prevails. Some of us have lost whole families. A grandfather accepts four flags in memory of his son, daughter-in-law, and two little grandchildren.

The Commission's most devastating finding confirms what we already know and will have to live with for the rest of our lives: this tragedy need never have happened. Here are highlights of the Commission's blunt and well-documented report:

The U.S. civil aviation security system is seriously flawed and has failed to provide the proper level of protection to the traveling public. The FAA is "far too reactive to problems instead of anticipating them" and pays far too little attention "to human factors and training." Pan Am's security lapses and the FAA's failure to enforce its own regulations followed a pattern that existed for months prior to Flight 103, on the actual day of the tragedy, and—notably—for nine months thereafter.

The report is filled with "shoulds." Congress should create the position of Assistant Secretary of Transportation for Security and Intelligence, an appointment with tenure to establish a measure of independence. Using FAA resources, the federal government should manage security at domestic airports through a system of federal security managers. And the United States should pursue a more vigorous counterterrorism policy. The State Department should conduct negotiations with foreign governments to permit U.S. carriers operating there to carry out FAA-required screening and other security precautions.

In addition, the FAA should launch a top priority R&D program to produce technology that will detect small amounts of plastic explosives at airports. Does the public have a right to be notified of threats to civil aviation? Yes, the report says, under certain circumstances. Victims of terrorist actions against the U.S. government should qualify for special financial compensation. And the victims themselves must be given higher priority. The State Department must ensure that families of victims receive prompt, humane, and courteous treatment and service in overseas disasters.

Despite our rising power as a lobbying group and the gratifying response of the President's Commission, some family members' philosophies conflict and personalities clash. A number of families split into a second group, Victims of Pan Am 103/Lockerbie. Miriam's stepmother and others spearhead it. Larry and I continue to support both groups. But it isn't long before I open my *Washington Post* one morning and discover a detailed mean-spirited feature story about the split. I'm incensed and publish a rebuttal on the *Post's* "Free for All" page. My point is that dissension eventually afflicts many organized groups of survivors because they are diverse human beings brought together solely by tragic events. But gossiping about the group conflicts takes attention away from our hard work to get the current legislation through Congress—a bill that will improve airline security and might even prevent another Pan Am 103. I also appeal to the *Post* to start attacking the Bush administration for its absolutely inexcusable current rapprochement with Iran and Syria. Both are on the State Department's list of countries that foster terrorism!

Despite the families' differences, their goals coincide and almost two years of painstaking lobbying pays off. Congress enacts the Federal Aviation Security Improvement Act of 1990. President Bush signs it into law on November 6. Senator Frank Lautenberg praises the families: "They've been tireless in their efforts to try to make sure that others are spared their grief. This legislation is a testament to their efforts and dedication."

Basically, the new law calls for speeding up development of technologies to detect explosives. Training standards for security personnel are to be upgraded, and federal aviation security managers are to be appointed within two years at all major airports—to replace private contractors now handling the job.

The new law also covers foreign air carriers. Those flying to and from the United States must comply with the same security measures required of U.S. carriers.

Warning provisions are to be strengthened. Better guidelines are to be established for notifying flight and cabin crews of a security threat. Better procedures are to be developed to notify passengers of credible terrorist threats.

The Secretary of State must publicize rewards offered for information leading to the arrest of terrorists. And the State Department must improve its procedures for dealing with the families of terrorist victims.

In the flush of triumph over the bill's passage, the VPAF103 newsletter reminds us of Hubert Humphrey's words: "Life's unfairness is not irrevocable. We can help balance the scales for others, if not always for ourselves."

But the most agonizing question remains unanswered: Who committed this crime? From the very day of the explosion, the U.S. government marshals the departments of State and Justice, the FBI, and the CIA and combines forces with the Scottish police and Scotland Yard.

Two months prior to the bombing of Pan Am 103, in October 1988, West German authorities raided a number of Frankfurt area residences where members of the Popular Front for the Liberation of Palestine-General Command (PFLP-GC) were holed up in "safe houses." Sixteen were arrested. Police discovered Toshiba radio–cassette recorders that had been tampered with—each one rigged as a bomb with a barometric trigger device, the kind of device used in previous attacks on civilian aircraft.

Inexplicably, by the end of October, all but three of the Palestinians had been released by the German courts. Intelligence sources determined that six bombs had been made. The German authorities found five. One was still missing. Possibly (although it's never been established), it was transported to the Mediterranean island of Malta, where it was packed in a bronze-colored Samsonite suitcase along with clothing purchased in Malta. The suitcase was placed aboard a Malta-to-Frankfurt flight. In Frankfurt, the unaccompanied interline luggage was transferred to Pan Am 103, a Boeing 727, for the European leg of the flight. I don't know why the bomb didn't explode on the flights from Malta and Frankfurt. Perhaps the crucial altitude criterion had not been met on those flight legs. The plane would later be traveling at a far higher altitude over the Atlantic. In London at Heathrow Airport, the luggage was transferred to a Boeing 747, the *Clipper-Maid of the Seas*, for Pan Am Flight 103's transoceanic flight bound for New York and Detroit.

The *Clipper-Maid of the Seas* took off with my beloved Miriam aboard, headed north and crossed the Scottish border. Thirty-seven minutes after takeoff, it blew up.

In 1991, after two years of worldwide investigation, the United States indicts two Libyan intelligence agents, Lamen Khalifa Fhimah and Abdel Basset Ali Megrahi. They are, respectively, the station chief and former security chief of Libyan Arab Airlines in Malta. It is believed that Megrahi is the senior officer in the Libyan intelligence service and director of its Center for Strategic Studies in Tripoli.

The brilliant investigative skills of the Americans, British, and Scottish cannot be emphasized too strongly. Combing almost a thousand square miles of Scottish countryside for clues, they found two significant fragments—each smaller than a fingernail. One turned out to be a piece of circuit board from a Swiss timing device that was sold to a high-level Libyan intelligence official; the other was a piece of the Toshiba radio–cassette circuit board. Investigators also found tiny bits of clothing that they traced to a shop in Malta—clothing that wound up stuffed into the Samsonite suitcase carrying the bomb.

Fhimah and Megrahi served only as the final means to an end. This was an act of state-sponsored sabotage. It is widely believed that three governments conspired in the bombing. Iran paid for it. Iran was seeking revenge for the accidental shooting down of an Iranian Airbus by the U.S. Navy missile cruiser *Vincennes*. Syria trained the terrorists. And the Libyan government carried out the act.

It is no mere speculation that Iran and Syria deal in terrorism. Our State Department has thoroughly documented Iran's terrorist activities as well as Syria's leading role in harboring and training terrorists for over a quarter of a century.

When nations officially foster mass murder, can there be any expectation of justice?

From the very day Miriam's plane exploded, Pan American World Airways chooses to take the adversarial role. Liability, not compassion, is their primary concern. Shortly after Miriam's death, we receive two ominous letters, as I believe every Pan Am 103 family did. One arrives from the chairman of the board of Pan Am, protesting the airline's innocence of wrongdoing. The tone is glib and defensive. The second letter comes from Pan Am's insurance carrier, U.S. Aviation Underwriters, offering to settle the case. If we accept their offer, we would absolve Pan Am of any wrongdoing.

Larry and I meet with Miriam's father and stepmother, and immediately agree not to accept the offer. First of all, Miriam's life is priceless. Having to articulate it in terms of monetary worth sends shivers up my spine. And we all agree that if we accept this money we are sending the message to Pan Am that it was blameless and bore no responsibility for allowing the bombing and for Miriam's death. We cannot do that. The four of us fervently believe that Pan Am did not fulfill its security responsibilities, willfully neglected them, and did not provide the security it had promised its passengers.

Early in 1989, Miriam's father and I join in a lawsuit against Pan Am with the prestigious New York aviation law firm Kreindler and Kreindler. The suit charges Pan Am with willful misconduct, fraud, and negligence in its security procedures. In pursuing the suit, the law firm sends me fifty-six "interrogatories"—categories of personal questions I'm to answer about Miriam: Her entire history—schools, grades, teachers; her salaries and supervisors of all her jobs; her illnesses, doctors, dentists, orthodontist, everything. What an ordeal. No trial date is set.

But these legal questions and answers don't tell who Miriam really was, so I write an impassioned ten-page essay about her, "Miriam Luby Wolfe, My Daughter, My Friend," and send it along with the interrogatories. And with this essay I begin a book about Miriam and our life together.

With the lawsuit, begins three years of obstruction and delaying tactics by Pan Am, as well as severe restrictions imposed on the victims by the presiding judge. But the victims triumph in the end. On July 10, 1992, a jury in U.S. District Court finds Pan Am guilty of willful misconduct. The trial outcome is one more example of the families banding together for strength, a force to be reckoned with. Highlights of the evidence, which supported the jury's willful misconduct verdict, are as follows:

Pan Am did not comply with FAA regulations, which require that unaccompanied interline luggage be hand-searched, not just X-rayed. Nor was the pilot informed that any unaccompanied bags were on board.

Because the airline was in financial trouble, it cut corners, severely limiting its security measures. Pan Am employed undertrained or completely untrained personnel and provided only minimal training. In Frankfurt, training materials, videos, and booklets were often in English—a language often not understood by the airline's X-ray operators and security inspection personnel stationed at the security check station. Sometimes the only training provided was a twenty-minute video in English! Security inspection personnel were recent hires, often unaware of the hazards they were searching for or trying to prevent.

Pan Am managers failed to disseminate U.S. State Department warnings of bomb threats to employees who could act upon them. The State Department's Toshiba Report warned of the existence of tampered cassette players housing plastic explosives and triggering devices. The report noted that German authorities had raided terrorist safe houses and found such devices. They provided descriptions and model numbers. A simple search of the several unaccompanied bags destined for Flight 103 would have uncovered the cassette bomb.

The U.S. Embassy in Helsinki received a call that a Pan Am flight from Frankfurt to the United States would be destroyed between December 5 and 19, 1988. At least some Pan Am security personnel in Frankfurt knew about it. The report was buried in other paperwork at Pan Am's Frankfurt station and later postdated to give the appearance that it had been received after Pan Am 103 was bombed.

Pan Am engaged in widespread fraudulent tactics, such as charging each passenger an extra ten dollars for "additional security," trumpeting this bonus feature in full-page newspaper ads. The truth? The extra fee went into the airline's general revenue fund and little, if any, found its way into improved security measures.

Pan Am also claimed it had dogs specially trained to detect explosives at JFK International Airport. Company executives appeared on television with these dogs. The truth? The animals were ordinary curs rented for the day from a Long Island kennel.

The day after the jury reaches its decision, the *Baltimore Sun* quotes me on its front page: "It's a moment of tremendous emotion.... I am flooded with the greatest sense of relief and vindication. The whole purpose of my joining the suit was so that the world would find out through a court of law about Pan Am's willful misconduct in its security. If Pan Am and its security arm, Alert, had done their jobs, followed the rules, and been sincere and followed the letter of the law spelled out by the FAA, my daughter, Miriam, would still be alive."

It will be three more years of delays and obstructions before Pan Am settles with the individual families. And vindication is bittersweet. Historically, executive suite villains get off scot-free. Let's examine for a moment the matter of corporate accountability. It is common knowledge that the main reason a business incorporates is to limit shareholders' liability to the value of the shares they hold. This, of course, is an important and necessary consideration for a business in raising entrepreneurial capital; if shareholder liability were not limited, nobody would buy stock. Corporate directors elected by the shareholders enjoy the same limited liabilities. When a corporation engages in the legal business activities prescribed by its prospectus, this limited liability is fitting and proper.

I am of the opinion that when a corporation is found guilty by a court of law of *willful* misconduct, then the protection of the corporate umbrella should not be available to the directors. The corporate entity has no will of its own. It has, instead, corporate policy and corporate will implemented consciously by its directors. In this case, Pan Am's policies encouraged employees to neglect their responsibilities, and far worse, these policies led to death and destruction. Why, then, aren't the directors and hands-on managers of a guilty corporate entity held criminally accountable?

A group of directors and executives brought dishonor and destruction to a prominent pioneer in the airline industry. Pan Am went out of business. But every so often, the company attempts to rise from the ashes of bankruptcy court to fly again. If there is any justice in the world, Pan Am will never again rise from its own ashes.

Where are we now? How much progress have we made? In some areas, very little. When TWA Flight 800 exploded in July 1996 I cried, I ached for the families. It was the same old story. Interminable delays. TWA personnel stalled in turning over the manifest and obstructed efforts of New York City officials to help the victims' families. On the plus side, only one week after the explosion, the U.S. Department of Justice and the U.S. Attorney's Office distributed a useful and compassionate booklet to the victims containing "Information and Assistance for Surviving Family Members."

The U.S. government is now taking a tougher stand against terrorists. I wish the media would too. It grieved me to see vast TV coverage and front-page stories on Timothy McVeigh, the convicted murderer of 168 innocents in Oklahoma City; the sympathetic pieces on the Unabomber; profiles of Palestinian terrorists and the two Libyans. Our media lionize criminals, who must surely conclude: See how much publicity they give us? They really take us seriously.

Airlines at only two U.S. airports in mid-1997 had high-tech equipment in place to detect chemical explosives. According to the VPAF103 newsletter *Truth Quest*, in August 1996 there were twenty-one other such detectors in use around the world. "Why does Manchester, England, have more state-of-the-art detectors than the entire United States?"

Our government is testing new technology in the building of airplanes—reinforced cargo holds to withstand the impact of an explosion. But don't look for airplanes containing such logical improvements any time soon.

Major U.S. airports have imposed increased security regarding luggage. Passengers must now produce a picture ID and unattended bags are confiscated.

Late in 1996, President Clinton signed the Terrorism Prevention Act into law. Among other provisions, it amends the Foreign Sovereign Immunities Act to allow U.S. citizens to sue governments that sponsor terrorism. As a result, many Pan Am families have joined together in a civil suit against Libya. This expanded law comes none too soon. In 1997 many Middle Eastern terrorist groups established cells in our country. The FBI has beefed up its staff and now has about 2,600 positions dedicated to counterterrorism.

In lobbying for the new antiterrorism law, Pan Am 103 families joined forces with other victims, including families of the Oklahoma City bombing, the World Trade Center bombing, the Korean Airlines 007 disaster, and the daughters of Leon Klinghoffer, whom terrorists murdered in 1985 aboard the cruise ship *Achille Lauro*.

Because Timothy McVeigh has been convicted and sentenced, victims of the Oklahoma City bombing have a sense of closure that can contribute to their healing. Thank God for that. And presumably any co-conspirators will also be caught and convicted. But we the victims of Pan Am 103 may forever be deprived of such closure and this measure of healing. Yes, the new law allows us to sue Libya. But a civil trial is not a criminal trial. Col. Moammar Gadhafi refuses to turn over the two Libyans to the United States or Scotland for trial. The Libyan government has bombarded the families of Pan Am with letters to evoke sympathy and protest its innocence. It is also demanding a trial in a neutral country or at the World Court in The Hague, Netherlands.

In mid-1998, the United States and Britain called Libya's bluff by agreeing to conduct the trial at The Hague under Scottish law with Scottish judges. In theory, Libya accepted the proposal. But as of this writing Gadhafi has still not turned over the suspects.

Since 1991 the U.N. has imposed economic sanctions against Libya to force the handing over of Fhimah and Megrahi, but to no avail. A group of U.S. senators and representatives, including Sen. Ted Kennedy, urges tougher sanctions—an oil embargo against Libya—but the U.N. will not agree to it. For years many U.N. member countries have persisted in buying Libyan oil and continue to flout the sanctions in other ways as well.

And let's not forget the most sinister part of this picture. These evil men, under the sponsorship of the Libyan government, are roaming around unpunished—free to commit additional terrorist crimes.

CHAPTER TWELVE

Grief and Healing

"GRANDMA? We sang 'You Are My Sunshine' in school today and I want you to sing it with me," Leah said. "But Mom told me it makes you cry."

I can't answer her. I'm fixing supper in our Honolulu apartment and suddenly I'm transported to my Severna Park kitchen. Miriam and I are doing dishes together and singing "You Are My Sunshine," harmonizing joyously as we so often did on so many songs. How I ache for those moments. My voice was strong then, but I hardly ever sing anymore. The notes come out ragged and my range has shrunk from disuse.

Abruptly, I'm returned to the present—to my grand-daughter waiting for my answer. I look down at her six-year-old's trusting eyes, trying so hard not to hurt me. "I'll sing with you," I say hesitantly.

Her sister, Alena, tiptoes into the kitchen, and in her small, sweet voice she says, "We're your sunshine now."

I gather them both in my arms. We sing.

When Miriam died, Craig and Alena were newborns, Ben and Leah would arrive two years later. I knew that eventually Jackie and Myrna would have to tell them the truth about how Auntie Miriam died. Now all four know. Eventually, baby Emily will, too. Both families live in Hawaii; they take so many plane trips to visit us and elsewhere, how do Jackie and Myrna reassure the kids that airplane travel is safe? They have explained that security is better now, and the subject does not seem to come up anymore. Alena and Leah ask to see pictures of Auntie Miriam as a child. They leaf through the albums. Miriam in her Red Riding Hood Halloween costume. Cuddling her cat and dog. Her fourth birthday party.

"Is Miriam in heaven?" Leah asks. Her mother assures her she is.

"Did you and Miriam ever have arguments?" Alena wants to know.

"We sure did—lots of them." These days Alena is flexing her nine-year-old's independence muscles, so she likes to hear that.

I can deal with all of this rationally now—at least most of the time. But in the beginning, well, that was a different story. For weeks after Miriam's death, my car became my private place of grief. Many mornings I'd pull into my office parking lot and have to sit in the car for ten minutes until I stopped crying and pulled myself together. My office was half a mile from BWI airport—so close that I'd see the planes coming and going every day. I couldn't get away from them. Their cold winking lights mocked me, reminded me that Miriam's plane didn't make it home. How I hated those winter nights, driving home in the sunset—the brilliant pinks and golds, the clouds haloed with reflected light. Miriam and I loved sunsets. We'd sit on a bench at our community dock, delighting in the flight of mallards and great blue herons as the sun settled over Cattail Creek.

Today I rarely cry in public. But those first two years I cried everywhere, especially in the supermarket, where I found myself bombarded with Mother's Day cards and birthday cards to daughters. At the mall, I walked into a shop where I'd bought Miriam a pumpkin-orange print dress that she loved. I intended to browse, but suddenly started sobbing. Two young clerks watched me with alarmed looks. I backed out of the store without a word.

Time heals and it doesn't. The pain doesn't fizz and disappear like an Alka-Seltzer plopped into a glass of water. And I don't expect it to. I remember my Grandma Elizabeth coming to the hospital to visit my terminally ill mother. Elegant in her little hat and gloves, ankles demurely crossed, Grandma sat next to Mother's bed day after day. After Mother died, Grandma's rosy cheeks turned pasty, her bright blue eyes dulled. She lived another decade, but she never recovered from her daughter's death.

Sigmund Freud lost his twenty-six-year-old daughter to a sudden illness. Ten years later he wrote a friend: "Although we know that...the acute stage of mourning will subside, we also know that we shall remain inconsolable and will never find a substitute."

Miriam's death so shattered my father that he went to see the rabbi of the temple where our family had been members for forty-seven years. He sought answers as a bereaved grandfather, not as a psychoanalyst. It was only after Father died that I found out he'd visited the rabbi. The news shocked me because, although he was deeply Jewish and the son of Orthodox Jews, he hated organized religion, and after my mother died he set foot in temple only for weddings and funerals. He went to see the rabbi, but he couldn't tell me about it. I think he worried I would see it as a weakness. He wanted to be strong for me and to set an example of strength. Which he did. He practiced psychiatry until nineteen days before he died at eighty-six. If he'd been able to lick the cancer, he would have taken a computer course, "because I don't want to be left out of the mainstream," he told us.

Thus, I shouldn't have been surprised that he too was looking for answers, to make some sense out of the loss of his granddaughter. Miriam and Grandpa Saul were so dear to each other. She gave him strength too. He learned from her— her exuberance, her eagerness to grow, to stretch her mind and explore. I once asked him:

"What keeps you going? What keeps you so optimistic?"

"Long ago," he said, "I decided I was going to live every day instead of die every day."

In some ways, I still can't accept the reality of Miriam's death. Sometimes I still wake up thinking this is preposterous, this couldn't have happened. I fantasize that she's still here. I construct a scenario that I had changed her to a different flight and she came home safely. The most painful one, the absolute worst is my wedding fantasy. I still can't pass a bridal shop without envisioning Miriam as a bride. I imagine the two of us flipping through bridal magazines. Or I hear a phone ring and it's my married Miriam calling to tell me she's pregnant. When she baby-sat for Rabbi and Fran Klensin's newborn son, I ambled across the street that Saturday night to see how things were going. Miriam answered the door with six-week-old Jacob slung on her hip, comfortably, as if he were her own second or third child. She would have made such a good mother. But I don't chastise myself for my fantasies. They float into my consciousness without invitation, unwelcome guests crashing my illusion of normalcy.

After Pan Am 103, the *Baltimore Jewish Times* raised astute questions: Why did the terrorists choose to plant a bomb on that particular flight? Because a large number of students were booked on it? Because the flight was scheduled so close to Christmas that the plane was expected to be full? Because a large number of kosher meals had been ordered? Or was it because the chief Nazi hunter for the U.S. State Department was on board? To this day we have no answers. No official ones, at any rate.

So I began to search for answers of another kind—mystical answers. Now please know that I am a thoroughly pragmatic, unmystical person. Yet here I was, after Miriam died, stepping through the door of an uncharted dimension in my life.

We were hitting tennis balls in the hot Sunday sun, the four of us—Larry and I, Myrna and Tim. It felt so good to be hitting well. And a few minutes of rare freedom for the kids with their new baby boy, our second grandchild. Suddenly a soft chuckle came from outside the court, where Harriet,

Tim's mother, was gently rocking Craig's stroller.

"Quick," she whispered, "you've got to see this." We all hurried over. Five-month-old Craig slept peacefully, his bare right foot resting on the stroller tray. On his chubby big toe sat a huge, exquisite monarch butterfly. We stood in silent awe as the butterfly lingered and lingered. A moment later, it gracefully darted off.

"It's Miriam," I said, "she's come to visit."

But my reaction embarrassed me. Was I behaving like a loony at a seance? Searching, searching, I dutifully flipped through my ever-growing stack of books on handling grief, yet gleaned no comfort. But one, written by a distinguished psychiatrist, caught my attention and I dove into it eagerly. It described cases of people who, under hypnosis, have recalled their former lives. The premise is that we live more than one life and this I can accept. Larry and I are so compatible that I'm convinced we knew each other in a previous life; on our first date I felt I'd known him forever.

So I was getting hooked on this book. It documented cases of small children who were able to speak a foreign language fluently without ever having been taught it or even exposed to someone who spoke that language. The conclusion was that they learned it in a former life. Okay, that sounded plausible. But then it described the case of a woman who had come back to earth about eight times—and with a lousy life each time! I laughed out loud. Apparently she just wasn't cutting it either on earth or in the Hereafter, so the Great CEO in the Sky— or, more likely, the assistant manager on cloud 72—handed her her walking papers. Laid off from the Great Beyond. I suppose she was told: "You'll just have to keep going back until you get it right."

So that book didn't help. But I also discovered *A World Beyond* by psychic Ruth Montgomery. Our loved ones, she says, aren't dead and gone forever, they're merely on "the Other Side"; they make choices of their own and can come back in spirit to be with us at different times or to live an entirely fresh life. Somehow there's a logic to this. It makes my reaction to the monarch butterfly seem less insane—even though Ms. Montgomery insists that humans don't change form in the afterlife. For instance, you can't come back as the family golden retriever. But this concept of our loved ones being on the Other Side is both enlightening and scary. If Miriam is on the Other Side, does she eavesdrop on Larry and me at will? Is she smiling at us? Is she passing judgment on me? Probably. Or has my daughter already returned to earth to live another life of her own?

Guilt—I seem to have been born with a second skin of it. We had to get rid of Miriam's dog, the fleas had taken over our house. As I sit at my desk, a shrill bark assaults my ears. New neighbors have moved in and their dog sounds just like Midnight. I brood. God is punishing me for getting rid of Midnight by reincarnating her in the dog next door.

I have been able to express my pain and find comfort in my friendship with Peggy and Ann. Nobody can understand what I'm going through except those who have also lost daughters on that fateful flight. We meet for lunch as often as we can. And we talk about our feelings and how the little things hurt so much. It is with Ann and Peggy that I can rage at the seemingly invulnerable terrorists. Most important, we remember the special times we had with our daughters. We laugh a lot too.

Six months after Miriam died, a neighbor called to tell me her eight-year-old daughter had broken her toe. She talked about it for ten minutes. I listened in silence, but when I hung up, I launched into a bitter argument with Larry.

"Miriam is dead and she's telling me about her daughter's toe? It isn't fair, why do I have to listen? My friends should stop telling me all this stuff about their daughters."

Larry tried to explain. "They love you and loved Miriam, but they can't censor their every word. You need their friendship and they have their lives too. Their children are what's important to them."

Anger bubbled up inside me like a malevolent hot spring. I ran upstairs to my desk and slammed myself into my chair. Burying my face in my arms, I burrowed into the basement of my mind. Was this to be my fate for the rest of my life—to listen stoically and grieve privately? Larry was right, of course, but back then I wasn't ready to accept the truth of it.

For over a year, I wept almost every time I got off the phone with my friends who have daughters. Not long ago, my neighbor and I talked about that particular phone conversation. Ironically, while she was telling me about the broken toe, she herself was wondering whether she should have said anything at all. Today my friends can tell me about their girls and I don't cringe inside quite the way I used to. I can bear it now. But sometimes I'm taken by surprise and I'm overwhelmed with acute sadness all over again. I was at a picnic when Julie arrived. She was a friend Miriam had grown up with, and I was so affected by her realness—by her being there and Miriam so blatantly absent—that tears overtook me behind my sunglasses. And I think she knew it.

On that afternoon I fell back down "the mountain," as my friend Ann calls it—the mountain of optimism and normalcy. Each day since Miriam died I claw my way up, groping for footholds that will regain a measure of my life back, grasping at every twig and branch of goodness in my life to help me cope better. Miriam is not coming back. But I can't survive dwelling on that thought. I survive on the knowledge that God gave her to me for twenty years.

On her birthday we visit her grave and lay our pebbles down among the many already there. How I would love to plant heather, her favorite flower, beside her headstone. But it's an Orthodox cemetery and only green shrubs are allowed. I've sometimes had a secret, almost overwhelming urge to plant the heather anyway. I can visualize arriving one day to find the entire cemetery covered with a glorious purple blanket. And on her birthday we always do something special. We go out to dinner with friends or we play tennis at night under the lights, and I look up at the starry sky and ask God to keep Miriam safe for me.

Searching for meaning in my life, I've plunged into new diversions. Masterpiece Theatre's superb *Middlemarch* led me to the novel. Where had this book been all my life? And I'm coming upon new distractions all the time. Weeding our little garden; the brilliant pink and fuchsia impatiens cheer me up. Watching the birds at our feeder just outside our kitchen window. Now there's a lifetime of entertainment for you. Chickadees, blue jays, Carolina wrens. In our yard, a flock of cedar waxwings stops by, alighting on Miriam's apple tree.

After a whole career mostly editing other authors, I'm now writing for myself. I've published nearly a dozen personal essays, most of them humorous.

Our grandson Craig once asked me: "Rosemary, why do you laugh so much?"

"Because it makes me feel better," I said.

My biggest adventure by far: Larry and I have embarked on a brand-new career: writing fiction together. We published a short story. We've written one mystery novel and have started a second one. We take writers' workshops and courses. What a challenge—and how much more difficult fiction is. We learn something new every day, and the harder we work, the more fun we have.

I've made another healing discovery: Our friends' children are now adults and are becoming our friends too. One sent us postcards from her travels to China and Europe; these cards made my day, her thinking of us when she was so far away. After I held a bridal shower for another young friend, she wrote me a letter in which she said, "I cherish your friendship." That was such a loving sentiment. There's a new and healthy dimension to all this. I've learned that Miriam's friends and our friends' children can enrich our lives too. They are more special people in this world for me and Larry to care about.

Miriam's close friends too enlarge our lives and that helps me to heal. Jake calls us on her birthday. Wendy and her husband visit with their little boys. Miriam's roommate Jessica has become our dear friend; she visits us and gives me as much moral support as I try to give her. And each time she performs in a new play—*Candide, Nunsense, Closer Than Ever, Arthur the Musical, Dames at Sea, The World Goes 'Round, Evita,* and many others—she makes a donation to the Miriam Luby Wolfe Scholarship Fund in honor of the cast and production staff.

It also dawned on me that as an editor and writer it was time to use my own resources for Miriam's benefit too. I began to publish her writings. Short stories, poems, essays, articles—in the *Washington Post, Cricket, Dramatics, Art Times: A Creative and Cultural Journal, Kids' Byline, Soap Opera Stars* and elsewhere. Each time I publish another of her pieces, a thrill of triumph goes through me. Each time I see her work in print, I feel I have immortalized her anew.

In a paper on Jerome Robbins for a dance class at Syracuse, Miriam wrote: "To be a true artist, one must challenge and defy convention, remain open-minded and always continue to learn." Her words provide a strong guiding principle for the remarkably gifted young men and women who receive awards that have been established in her memory. At Temple Beth Shalom, the Miriam Luby Wolfe Scholarship Fund is open to both high school and elementary school students who are gifted academically and/or in the arts and have a strong sense of community, Jewish life, and the family. Sometimes two winners are chosen in one year. One was Laura, an eight-year-old who sings and dances. Her mother just happened to have performed in *The Music Man* with Miriam in 1986; she was pregnant with Laura at the time! The awards committee didn't know this, of course. Just an eerie coincidence. Each winner of this award is so exceptional that I draw a great measure of peace in knowing they are perpetuating Miriam's values and ideals. Michael spent his senior year of high school at New York University. Miriam was Paul's camp counselor and he used his scholarship toward tuition at the University of

Pennsylvania, where he planned to minor in Judaic Studies. Rachel used her award for a trip to Israel.

At Severna Park High, the English Department renamed its annual award for seniors the Miriam Luby Wolfe Memorial English Award. The recipients have touched my heart with their excellence. Among them are a poet and a Shakespeare scholar.

Children's Theatre of Annapolis has also presented scholarships in her memory to students gifted in the performing arts.

My days are brightened and buoyed up by her friends who have showered us with poems written about her, a song composed for her, and a friend who named his new cat Luby.

Myrna and Jackie have been a great source of comfort to me. They call me their "stepmom" and at first I was careful to call them my stepdaughters. But it wasn't long before I yearned to call them "daughter." Would they be offended, I wondered. But they're not in the least, probably because I'm their friend and have never tried to take their mother's place. (Ironically, one of the many things we have in common is the fact that both of our mothers died of cancer at age forty-eight.) I did have one problem, though. At first I also wondered whether calling them "daughter" was in some way a betrayal of Miriam. I decided it wasn't. It's merely another symbol of how much I miss her.

When we're not all in Hawaii together, Larry and I call the girls every Sunday. Just talking to them cheers me up and makes me feel renewed, less deprived, less bereft. And talking to our grandchildren infuses me with happiness. Being able to talk about "our kids," "our girls" gives me a new lease on life. I feel like a new person. And Larry's willingness to share them with me is limitless, because that's the kind of person he is. Giving is a way of life for him.

Larry, with his humor and positive outlook, is my best friend, my mainstay. He is what we call a *mensch* in Yiddish, a loving, giving man. He's a sympathetic listener and appreciates my talking about Miriam. He lets me cry as much as I need to;

it's very hard for him to see me suffering, but he never makes me feel I should keep my anguish to myself because it makes *him* uncomfortable.

In the spring of 1993, Myrna and Tim called to tell us that they were moving from Maryland to Molokai, an outer island of Hawaii. They are both teachers and already had jobs. Tim is an athlete and wanted to be in a warm climate. Myrna wanted to be near her sister. But before the news was even out of Myrna's mouth, I began sobbing. Here comes another loss, I thought. The move was what the kids wanted and needed to do. But for three days I cried as if I'd lost another daughter.

Their move propelled Larry and me to take early retirement near the end of that year to spend the winters in Hawaii. We could manage it, we had our health, we'd be closer to our kids, and our four grandchildren would get to know us.

What I didn't count on was the shock of leaving my job. I had worked for thirty-four years, but only six at Westinghouse and I wasn't really geared to quit. A subtle new form of grieving settled over me as I thought about my friends and colleagues at work, my managers, whom I really liked, and the undeniable excitement and stimulation of the corporate climate. My identity had been wrenched from me, I was no longer a professional editor and writer. And catapulted into the quiet of our house, I now had too much time to brood about Miriam. She was dead almost five years, but that made no difference. It seemed like yesterday.

We arrived in balmy Hawaii with its caressing trade winds on December 1. Jackie and her family greeted us at the airport with fragrant plumeria leis and hugs and kisses. But as we neared December 21, the fifth anniversary of Pan Am 103, an additional sense of isolation overtook me.

I have always been deeply affected by the passage of seasons. Every December for as long as I can remember, I would weave my way through rush hour traffic in darkness, gratefully aware on the twenty-first of the month that the days would now start growing longer. But now December 21 is a sinister day. The weeks leading up to it loom heavy as I helplessly re-hash the night Miriam died. I want to forget, but the horror wraps around me like a python and smothers me with its reality. The shortest day of the year, the longest night, the onset of winter. On December 21, 1988, winter settled into my soul.

December of 1993 was particularly painful. The families of Pan Am 103 were meeting with President Clinton at Arlington National Cemetery to lay the cornerstone for a memorial. The bombing was considered an act of terrorism against the government of the United States. The memorial would be a Scottish "cairn," a fifteen-foot-high monument of 270 red, brick-shaped stones, one for each victim, donated by the Scottish government and mined from a quarry near Lockerbie. Never had I felt so alone. I wanted to be with Ann and Peggy and the other families to mourn our children. So what did I do to console myself?

I walked around the corner from our apartment to a Korean beauty parlor to get my hair done. On December 21 at 10 A.M. I engaged in a very unsolemn conversation with the lady proprietor.

"My hair won't stay set in this tropical climate," I complained.

"Of course," she lectured me. "Wrong hairdo for Hawaii. I cut it short, much better, no more set."

"Really?" I asked uneasily. But she had already started snipping. Moments later, I looked like a fifty-eight-year-old pixie.

That night I confided in Jackie: "My first new hairdo in fourteen years. Miriam encouraged me." Then I blushed for saying something so weird. But she laughed. "Like Miriam was telling you, 'Mom, go for it!'"

Jackie's reaction amazed me. She didn't think I was crazy. Her complete understanding washed over me like a gentle wave. It was okay for me to be in Hawaii instead of at Arlington. On December 21, as much as we could manage it, Miriam and I were together after all.

I spend a good and satisfying share of my life with my nose in dictionaries and my thesaurus. In writing this book, struggling not to be repetitive, I've made a really strange discovery: that there aren't many synonyms in the English language for "cry." One can say "weep" or "sob" or "shed tears," or "mourn," but then you start running out of words. Maybe there's a message in this, a basic truth that emerges through thousands of years of our language's evolution. Maybe after we allow ourselves all the crying we need to—or perhaps despite the crying that helps us—we need to turn our attention, no matter how much we hurt, to living the best way we can.

In *A Grief Observed*, C.S. Lewis writes about the death of his young wife: "Passionate grief does not link us with the dead but cuts us off from them.... It is just at those moments when I feel least sorrow—getting into my morning bath is one of them—that H. rushes upon my mind in her full reality... Not, as in my worst moments, all foreshortened and patheticized and solemnized by miseries, but as she is in her own right. That is good and tonic."

The oddest thing about this quote is that Miriam recorded it in one of her London diaries. Why, in a time of such happiness, was she drawn to this sentiment? I get chills when I read it, because it speaks directly to me. And it confirms my feeling that she had a mystical side to her.

In October 1993, I reached a milestone. I published an article in *McCall's* entitled "Please Remember My Daughter." The day of publication gave me a sense of achievement like no other since she died. Now millions of readers throughout the world knew about my child. The article ended with Miriam's own words, her personal guidelines for her life.

The force of her personality came through with such power that the response to the article surprised even me. A high school senior in Maryland concluded her graduation valedictory address with Miriam's words. A woman in Israel invited me and Larry to come visit and even gave us her phone number. A teacher in Ohio called to say Miriam's story had given her

courage and strength—strength that she sorely needed, because this single Caucasian woman had adopted an African-
American baby and much of her family had disowned her afterward. The editor of *McCall's* wrote to me:

"Reading about Miriam has had a very big effect on my
life—I really carry her wisdom with me every day now. I had
gotten away from seeing the joy of each day and she has re-
stored my spirit. What a fabulous legacy."

What were Miriam's words that stoked the fires of so many
people? They were her own prescription for living, her personal philosophy, which I myself only discovered in one of her
London notebooks. It is such profound advice that it speaks to
all of us. But it speaks especially to me. With these words, my
daughter has taken me by the hand and led me into a healing
place:

"There are times when the 'poor me' mood is upon us;
we're overwhelmed by all the troubles we have to face. This is
especially likely to happen when we have begun to try to
change our thinking about ourselves and our relation to others. We may, at first, become too analytical and try to solve too
much at once. For this frame of mind there is an almost infal-
lible prescription: to empty our minds of all thoughts but
one—today and how to use it. This day is mine. It is unique.
Nobody in the world has one exactly like it. It holds the sum
of all my past experience and all my future potential."

CHAPTER THIRTEEN

The Terrorists Haven't Won

In the depth of winter, I finally learned that within me there lay an invincible summer.

—Albert Camus

WHEN TWA Flight 800 exploded in a fireball off Long Island, I could not watch the news reports. For two days I was in a state of denial. My chest was tight, my throat was constricted. I felt like I was choking. Over and over on TV, I saw the shots of Pan Am Flight 103 lying in the Scottish countryside, a broken, dead beast. And I was being dragged back nearly eight years to relive my own horror.

My heart ached for those families. So many similarities to Pan Am 103. So many children on board. Losing a child is the ultimate hell. There is no getting over it. So much love, so much potential destroyed. To this day the experts don't know what caused TWA 800 to explode, but I knew what lay ahead for those TWA families. The moment Miriam died, I became an unwilling public figure. We all did, all of us who waited that night beside phones and in airports for our loved ones who would never come home.

The night after my daughter died, I woke up screaming from a bone-chilling nightmare. In the dream, I was huddled with my grieving family at her graveside as we were burying her. Suddenly, a sinister band of men, wearing camouflage uniforms and carrying machine guns, poured out of a bus and came thundering toward us. It was a terrifying image. For

169

nearly five years, I had these grotesque dreams that wouldn't let me rest.

My nightmares were not confined to the night. A generalized anxiety, a foreboding lurks inside me still, hovers over me, shadows me throughout my day. Will the terrorists plant a bomb on the next plane I travel on? Or will it happen on the metro as I benignly head for a day of sightseeing in Washington?

Even worse is the daily nightmare of living without Miriam. Not having her to talk to. I hear Bette Midler sing "The Rose" on the radio; I have a tape of Miriam singing "The Rose," so sweetly, so exquisitely it makes me cry. I can no longer tolerate one of my favorite pieces of music, "Pomp and Circumstance," because now it represents the college graduation Miriam was denied.

My dreams aren't always nightmares. Miriam is often in my dreams—always alive and well, perky and exuberant, vigorously pursuing her daily life. And paired with this nighttime fantasy is an obsessive thought that keeps pressing against my skull, logical and irrational all at once: Okay, I've proved that I'm strong; I can handle suffering; I can function and be productive; I continue to nurture my husband and family. I've been tested and I passed. Now I want her back.

But it isn't going to happen, not in this life. So I content myself with the next best thing: perpetuating her legacy, which continues to surge like ocean waves on the world. Her charisma left indelible impressions. Two friends and a cousin have named their babies after her. After I published one of her short stories in *Cricket*, an eight-year-old from Minnesota wrote to say that in the year she'd had her subscription, Miriam's story was one of her two favorites. So my daughter's impact weaves through new lives, touching the hearts and souls of yet another generation.

I often wonder—what would my beloved daughter be doing if she were still here? She'd have graduated from Syracuse in 1990. She'd be performing—singing, dancing, acting.

She'd be directing plays. Perhaps she would have even

started her own theater company by now (she was already studying grantsmanship). She planned to write, direct, and produce; do tours, workshops, political issue theater. She'd be teaching acting to children, she'd be writing plays and poems. She'd be a professional writer, perhaps for a newspaper. In London she made a list of "Things I Really Want To Do: Become a therapist some day. Work in a drug/alcohol rehab center. Teach high school kids and work with toddlers. Study government and politics." Most likely she'd be doing a fair share of all these things by now.

What else might Miriam be doing? She'd be living in an apartment in New York or Chicago. She'd be visiting Larry and me, playing Big Boggle with us—and winning. She'd be hugging me, laying her head on my shoulder, or wanting me to hear "just this one song" or "just this poem" even though it was midnight. She'd be debating with Larry or rolling her eyes at one of his puns. She might be married—and even a mother by now.

We received a few condolence notes saying the blowing up of Pan Am 103 was "God's will" and "Everything happens for a reason." Some people need to believe that for their own peace of mind. I don't believe it for a minute. The very idea strikes me as not only outrageous, but blasphemous, an injustice to God.

Nevertheless, I have raged in my private moments, asking myself the same questions that Rabbi Klensin raised in his eulogy. How could a good, just, and loving God have let this happen? At first, engulfed in self-pity, I cried, "Why me?" And then, after much deliberation, I saw the question as "Why them?" There were babies on that plane and more than a hundred passengers in their twenties. Can it be God's will to put such a loving, gifted creature as Miriam on this earth and then take her away before she has reached her bloom and full potential?

The night Miriam died, for a fleeting moment I told myself there is no God. But I immediately squashed that thought—mostly in fear that if I persisted in voicing it, I would bring even greater devastation down on myself. In succeeding days, the heretical thought revisited me, refusing to go away; it festered and infected my logical thinking. Again I asked myself: Could He be a just and loving God if He allowed a Pan Am 103 to happen? Is there a God at all? And what has become of life's natural rhythm and the harmony of His heavenly universe?

But I already know the answer. It is not a flawed blueprint. It's the terrible wrongs that evil men contrive to disrupt His glorious plan for a harmonious existence. There must be a God, because He gave me Larry and Jackie and Myrna and Rodney and Tim and our grandchildren. Alena was born the week of Miriam's twentieth birthday. Craig, five weeks old, slept in Myrna's arms in our living room as we sat *shivah*. And now we have our precious Ben, Leah, and Emily too.

Among the hundreds of friends, family members, and even the most remote acquaintances who came to our house, there wasn't one who wasn't thinking: Thank God Rosemary has Larry. So true. And God has been good to me in giving me all our cherished relatives—and dear friends, who make up our extended family.

When your only child has been murdered, does grief include a lifetime of bitterness? It inflames me when I read in the papers about monster parents like the South Carolina mother who deliberately drowned her two small sons. By what right, by what higher authority, did that mother deserve her children when I, who was so loving and nurturing, have been deprived of mine? But that train of thought won't get me anywhere. Evil exists in the world; it's a fact of life. At Temple Beth Shalom, we pray, "May the time not be distant, O God, when...unbelief shall disappear and error be no more...when corruption and evil shall give way to integrity and goodness...." Until such time, there will be evil in the world—and my raging against monster parents and the injustice of it all is self-defeating.

On the High Holy Days, for years after Miriam's death, I sat in temple crying more than meditating, crying more than singing, crying more than praying. I'm surrounded by Miriam's friends from religious school, Confirmation, and Youth Group. I cry because they're here and she isn't. I read my prayer book. It tells us to forgive, forgive, forgive. But I can't forgive the terrorists. I never will.

This year I cried a little less—because of one passage in the prayer book. It spoke of God leading our people out of Egypt to serve Him in freedom. "Full of joy, Moses, and Miriam, and all Israel sang...." Somehow, reading that passage, in the very tangible speaking of Miriam's name, I felt renewed.

In every service we recite the Kaddish, the mourners' prayer. The origins of the Kaddish are mysterious. According to *Gates of Prayer*, angels are said to have brought it down from heaven. The Kaddish never acknowledges death. Instead, it permits the blossom, which has fallen from the tree of humankind, to flower and grow again in the human heart. The Kaddish mentions neither death nor grief. Instead, it extols the glory of God. It represents a moral triumph for the mourner because the prayer turns attention away from our inwardness, away from our individual sorrow to focus on the glory of God and the hope for a better life for all. And I try to remember our Yom Kippur memorial book's words: "We do our best homage to our dead when we live our lives most fully, even in the shadow of our loss. For each of our lives is worth the life of the whole world."

In his Kol Nidre sermon on Yom Kippur last year, Rabbi Klensin announced that one of our young congregants, a sixteen-year-old girl, had been killed that week. And then he told us a story about the great violinist Yitzak Perlman—a man who has overcome severe physical handicaps to share his gift with the world. During a major concert, Mr. Perlman began playing, when suddenly one of his violin strings snapped. The conductor signaled the orchestra to stop. The packed house sat hushed. Everyone expected Mr. Perlman to ask for another

violin or at least a new string. But he didn't. He motioned for
the conductor to continue and played the entire concert mi-
nus the broken string. Afterward, he was asked why he didn't
call for a substitute violin or at least another string. Yitzak
Perlman replied:

"We make music with what we have, and when that's gone,
we must make music with what we have left."

Where will I find the music that will give me peace?
Would my fears and nightmares end if the Libyans who placed
the bomb on Pan Am 103 were in prison and the heads of the
governments responsible were punished? Partly, but only
partly, because now terrorism has invaded American soil too.
With the bombings of Oklahoma City, the World Trade Center, and Centennial Olympic Park in Atlanta, it is now part of
our local criminal landscape. Is there anything at all the aver-
age citizen can do? At times I am overwhelmed by a sense of
helplessness.

Have the terrorists defeated me personally? No—because
I am Miriam's mother. She remains a part of my very soul. She
nurtures me. Her memory blooms richly in all who knew her.
No terrorist can destroy that. Difficult as it is for me at times,
I will continue to perpetuate her joyful outlook, to find within
me Camus' "invincible summer." Miriam herself was a crusad-
er, she was determined to make the world a better place, but
at the same time she had a passionate appreciation of God's
gifts to us and an innocent confidence, as did Anne Frank, in
the basic goodness of people.

An acid irony eats at me: I live in a world so imperfect that
it took her from me. But in one of Miriam's journals, returned
to me by the Scottish police, she wrote about her visit to Wales
with an optimism that sustains me every hour of my life:

"The sky was bluer today, the sun was yellower today, and
the whole of the earth seemed to be rejoicing in its own per-
fection."